Sustainable Growth and Profits

Managing Your Innovation Strategy, Organization, and Initiatives

Magnus Penker,

Peter Junermark and Sten Jacobson

Contents

FOREWORD BY PROF JOHAN ROOS 8
FOREWORD BY KENNETH CARL RAMOS. 9
ACKNOWLEDGMENTS 11

CHAPTER 1 . . . .*15*
THE COMPLETE GUIDE TO BUSINESS INNOVATION,
VOLUMES 1 TO 5 15

CHAPTER 2 . . . .*21*
INTRODUCTION TO VOLUME 5:
SUSTAINABLE GROWTH AND PROFITS 21

CHAPTER 3 . . . .*29*
THE CHANGING ROLE OF STRATEGY. 29
   3.1   *Innovation Strategies* *29*
   3.2   *Change is the New Constant for innovation strategies* *31*
   3.3   *Innovation strategy for Sustainable development* *35*
   3.4   *Linking Innovation Strategy to Imperative External Requirements* *35*
   3.5   *Strategies for the Unknown* *37*
   3.5.1.1 *Best Fit*. *41*
   3.5.1.2 *Best in Class* *42*
   3.5.1.3 *Resource-Based View* *42*

CHAPTER 4 . . . .*45*
THE CHANGING ROLE
OF LEADERSHIP AND CULTURE. 45
   4.1   *SMEs and Large Organizations*. *47*
   4.2   *Many Layers*. *48*
   4.3   *Leading with Paradoxes*. *49*
   4.3.1.1 *The Dr Winterkorn Paradox*. *49*

4.3.1.2	The Too-Big-to-Fail Paradox	49
4.3.1.3	The Uber Uber Alles Paradox	50
4.3.1.4	The Lean and the Mauser Paradox	51
4.4	Diverse Teams	51
4.5	Leading with Purpose	54
4.5.1.1	Understand the difference between Capability and Competence	57
4.5.1.2	Use Personas to build successful innovation organizations	58
4.5.1.3	Learning Personas	59
4.5.1.4	Organizational Personas	60
4.5.1.5	Building Personas	60
4.6	Understanding Social Bias and the Stages of Group Development	61

CHAPTER 5 .... **65**

EXTERNAL ANALYSIS 65

5.1	Global Key Drivers - The PESTLED Framework	66
5.1.1.1	Political forces	67
5.1.1.2	Economical forces	67
5.1.1.3	Social forces	67
5.1.1.4	Technological forces	68
5.1.1.5	Legal forces	68
5.1.1.6	Environmental forces	69
5.1.1.7	Demographic forces	69
5.2	The Maturity of a Market – S-Curve analysis	70
5.2.1	Reinventing a Market	72
5.2.2	Expanding and Redefining a Market	73
5.3	The Collaborative Landscape - The Six Driving Industry Forces	73

CHAPTER 6

INTERNAL ANALYSIS 77

6.1	How to Assess Aspiration and Ability for Change and Innovation	78
6.2	Why Innovate?	81
6.3	What to Innovate?	81
6.4	How to Innovate?	82
6.5	Where to Innovate?	83
6.6	When to Innovate?	83
6.7	The Wheel of Innovation	83
6.7.1.1	The Nomenclature	86
6.7.1.2	Innovation Aspect: M – Value Proposition (What)	87
6.7.1.3	Innovation Aspect: M E – Platform	87

6.7.1.4   *Innovation Aspect: M E – Products* *88*

6.7.1.5   *Innovation Aspect: M E – Services*. *88*

6.7.1.6   *Innovation Aspect: E – Customer Insights (Who)*. *89*

6.7.1.7   *Innovation Aspect: P E – Customer Experience* *89*

6.7.1.8   *Innovation Aspect: P E – Customer Engagement* *89*

6.7.1.9   *Innovation Aspect: P E – Value Capture*. *90*

6.7.1.10   *Innovation Aspect: P – Process (How)* *90*

6.7.1.11   *Innovation Aspect: P I – Organization*. *91*

6.7.1.12   *Innovation Aspect: P I – Learning Capabilities* *91*

6.7.1.13   *Innovation Aspect: P I – Supply* *91*

6.7.1.14   *Innovation Aspect: I – Channel (Where)* *91*

6.7.1.15   *Innovation Aspect: M I – Linkages*. *92*

6.7.1.16   *Innovation Aspect: M I – Openness* *92*

6.7.1.17   *Innovation Aspect: M I – Brand*. *93*

6.8   *Identifying the Business Model and Strategic Options* *93*

6.8.1   *Understanding the Internal Context*. *93*

6.8.2   *Revise Strategic Direction Based on Internal and External Context* *96*

6.8.3   *Validate Current Strategic Options, and Generate New Ones*. *97*

6.8.4   *Evaluate Strategic Options*. *100*

6.8.5   *Prioritize Strategic External and Internal Initiatives in Each Horizon* *102*

6.8.5.1   *Initiatives in Horizons*. *102*

6.8.6   *Establish a Change Program to Support Strategic Change* *102*

6.9   *Linking External and Internal Analysis to Business Development – Using the* . .
            VMOST Framework *103*

CHAPTER 7 . . . . **105**

STRATEGIC INITIATIVES AND PLATFORM MANAGEMENT. . .105

7.1   *Managing strategic initiatives and Innovation projects* *105*

7.2   *Managing Platform Development* *109*

CHAPTER 8 . . . . **113**

LEADING CHANGE FOR INNOVATION **113**

8.1   *Manage the challenges through UPACS* *113*

8.2   *Manage your Stakeholders for Radical Innovation*. *115*

8.3   *Develop the right team(s)* *117*

CHAPTER 9 . . . . **121**

ORGANIZATIONAL DESIGN **121**

9.1   *Setting Strategic Goals and Making the Correct Design Choices*. *122*

9.2   *Organizational Principles for Innovation Centers* *124*

CHAPTER 10

ARTIFICIAL INTELLIGENCE AND INNOVATION – AN EXECUTIVE'S TECH GUIDE BEYOND RHETORIC 127

10.1   *What Is Artificial Intelligence and Machine Learning,*
          and How Does It Work? *129*

10.1.1.1 *The Brain* *129*

10.1.1.2 *The Black Box* *130*

10.1.1.3 *Design: Hidden Layers* *132*

10.1.1.4 *Design: The Activation Function.* *133*

10.1.1.5 *Design: Backward Propagation of*
          Errors and Gradient Descent *133*

10.1.1.6 *Design: Recurrent Neural Network* *134*

10.2   *What Artificial Intelligence and Deep Learning Can Do for You* *134*

10.2.1.1 *More Applications.* *135*

10.2.1.2 *Intersectional Thinking* *136*

10.2.1.3 *Level of Applications.* *136*

10.2.1.4 *Innovation and AI* *137*

10.3   *How Artificial Intelligence Can Be Used to Reinvent Your Business Model* . . *139*

10.4   *Limitations and Business Risk of Using AI and Machine Leaning in Business* . .
          Development. *141*

10.5   *When Will "The Terminator" Be a Reality?* *143*

CHAPTER 11 . . . . *147*

EPILOGUE AND CONCLUSIONS 147

REFERENCE LIST 151

ABOUT THE AUTHORS 155

FOREWORD BY PROF JOHAN ROOS

The American businesswoman Mary Kay Ash famously said that there are three types of people in this world: those who make things happen, those who watch things happen and those who wonder what happened. This book speaks about the first type and urges the second to stop watching and start innovating.

Magnus Penker admits upfront that no one has any idea where the current technological advancements may lead us, but his message is clear: make yourself a proper innovation strategy. He speaks with the authority that comes from substantial empirical evidence and a good grasp of the concepts.

In this book we learn in details about what successful innovators do based on much data from the innovative 360 model of innovation strategy. Because of its quickly growing importance, we also learn about how AI technology is already driving business model innovation across industries.

Let's get into the driving seat.

Johan Roos, February 2018

Professor of General Management and Strategy, Hult International Business School. Author of Disrupting Innovation Through Collaborative Competitions (2017), Bridging the Gender Gap (2014), and co-inventor of LEGO® Serious Play®.

FOREWORD BY KENNETH CARL RAMOS

In Swedish, to say that you are passionate about something is to say that you "burn for it". Swedes burn for innovation as well as technical creativity. This book clarifies, defines, as well as redefines what organizations must do to strike the tangible balance between innovation and producing "risk adjusted returns" or quite simply quantifiable results. Rarely has the concept of diminishing returns been more profound as the current technological (and Fourth Industrial) revolutionary wave ripples across the planet. As blockchain, AI, robotics and biological systems are all moving across the space & time continuum it would appear that a major strategic inflection point is right around the corner. Those companies unprepared to successfully negotiate this intersection as they continue to run their respective business models in the exact same manner they did over the space of many years will probably not survive. Those companies who quickly embrace, adapt, and ultimately leverage these changes will dramatically increase the probability of building out a successful, sustainable business model.

I am American, a financial advisor, and have worked at several large firms throughout my career. I spent the last three years of my career building a pipeline between New York and the Nordics as I observed that the region was indeed going through a renaissance within the technology and life science arenas. I have been to Sweden, Finland, Norway, and Iceland a total of six times during this time frame and have immersed myself in the Swedish language, culture, and mindset. I ultimately met Mr. Penker last year in New York. I observed that the methodology he and the Innovation 360 team laid out was sound and could be applied to almost any industry. Innovation 360 creates the blueprint from which a given company may take their infrastructure from the ideation to the governance stage all while maintaining rigid business metrics.

I bring value to the table by building meaningful long-term relationships

9

through patience, perseverance, and cultural immersion. Raising awareness about innovative companies coming out of Sweden & elsewhere in the Nordics is my most profound passion which I truly "burn for." This book lays out a process in a very Nordic logical & systematic manner that a given company can implement through innovation. It may very well help you to define and successfully negotiate the rapidly changing technological environment which is causing mass disruption across the business spectrum.

Kenneth Carl Ramos, February 6, 2018

ACKNOWLEDGMENTS

In writing this five-volume series, I've relied heavily on the work of theorists, consultants, CEOs, project managers, and many, many other innovative thinkers across the decades. They are far too many to name, but they deserve recognition. I'd like to take a moment now to sincerely thank everyone who has brought this group of innovation manuals to fruition.

As I've said and seen countless times, ideas come into the world on their own schedule, often to many people at once who are oceans apart and working in disconnected fields. I want to personally thank everyone who shared in the formation of the ideas presented here, and I hope to live long enough to say so to each of you in person.

For now, I would like to recognize a few of the individuals who did truly extraordinary work to encapsulate the concepts from this volume in their present form.

First of all, my thanks go out to Prof. Philip Kotler, in the International Marketing Department at the Kellogg School of Management, Northwestern University. Your words have been extremely inspirational and encouraging in prompting me to publish my key findings and methodology. Then I want to thank Scott McNealy, founder of Sun Microsystems, for sharing his leadership experience and thoughts on running an innovation center that resulted in some of the most profound innovations in modern history.

I also send my special appreciation to the entire team at Innovation360. I'm sure they know that they have my profound respect for their role in helping bring new ideas into the world. I would also like to include those outside the company who have made valuable contributions to the presentation of this series, such as Dragan Bilic and Henrik Lundblad for their graphical work, and Sasha Viasasha and Annginette Anderson for their editorial help.

Next, my gratitude goes out to our clients and the greater network of independent

Innovation360 licensed practitioners who are working in the field right now to support the next generation of innovators. I would especially like to mention Maurizio Grassi for his contribution regarding cryptocurrencies and blockchain. I also want to mention Niclas Claesson, Julia Doria, Martin Hultqvist, Paulo Malta, Thierry Bernicard, Christopher Michael, Renee Reynolds, Farhan Majeed, Peter Popovics, Khaled Adas, Sofie Lindblom, Tanya Sasivanij, Saif Amer, Agnes Sävenstedt, Jens Nilsson, Peet van Biljon and Allan Ashok for their profound and important contributions.

Finally, I want to thank my coauthors Peter Junermark and Sten Jacobson.

Magnus Penker

Stockholm, Sweden

March 2018

CHAPTER 1

THE COMPLETE GUIDE TO BUSINESS INNOVATION, VOLUMES 1 TO 5

The past can no longer be a predictor. The forces reshaping global culture have become so sweeping and multifaceted that a company's past successes have lost their statistical weight in projections of what is most likely to happen next.

There have been only a few other historical precedents of times like the one we are in now, where the post-change world looks absolutely nothing like the world before.

» *The World's Four Industrial Revolutions*

We are now living in the midst of the Fourth Industrial Revolution, fundamentally rewriting the rules of how we live, work, and relate to one another. Somewhere in the world right now, there is most probably a working prototype of an innovation that will be as profound as the internet or self-aware AI.

The World Economic Forum introduced this conceptual framework for global development in 2016, but the evidence has been right in front of us for a great deal longer.

The First Industrial Revolution in the 18th century transformed the world of work from animal-powered labor to mechanical drivers. The Second in the 19th century brought to bear electricity and previously unimagined economies of scale. The Third in the 20th century transferred industrial logistical control to computers and automation.

Now, in the 21st century, and in the midst of the Fourth industrial revolution, we are witnessing the convergence of all past advances in power and energy. Mechanical devices, electricity, and networked computers are merging with biological systems and are projected to outperforming the human brain within a decade or two.

And even more thought provoking would be to ask ourselves, will there be a Fifth industrial revolution in the future? Most likely?

But honestly, no one has any idea where this will lead us.

» *Finding a successful Path Ahead*

So, for now, let's hope we manage to control and guide this development for the good as opposed to the bad/evil opportunities it inevitably will provide to our planet.

In its scale, scope, and complexity, the Fourth industrial revolution is ushering in a world unlike anything we have experienced in the past. Like the world of quantum mechanics, common sense does not apply to uncommon environments. While we cannot know how this will unfold on the macro level, each organization can take control of its own destiny by defining its innovation strategy.

In order for their organization to play a consequential role in the sweeping changes swirling all around it and to benefit from the opportunities they present, leaders must follow a praxis that is integrated, comprehensive, and involves all external and internal stakeholders.

If there are any omissions or vulnerabilities in the foundations of their business strategy, market forces will simply tear it apart. Successful leaders therefore adhere to methodologies that aligns strategy, leadership styles, internal culture, untapped capabilities, and adaptable competencies.

» *Control your destiny through a Comprehensive Innovation Strategy*

Solid research indicates that a coordinated innovation strategy will be the key to success in building innovative, sustainable business models that thrive amid the turbulent times ahead. Organizations that aspire to persistent relevancy need a true, reliable, and easily measurable 360-degree understanding of what just happened, what is happening at the moment, and which potential futures are most likely to occur.

Entrepreneur and international innovation expert Magnus Penker built the Innovation360 Group to offer businesses a pathway for achieving that understanding. Penker's journey began with a deceptively simple question: "Why do some innovative firms change the world while others struggle to survive?" Based on analysis of data from thousands of businesses, Penker concluded that it is not a matter of luck, although timing does matter. And it's not just talent, a well-connected board, or intelligent funding choices.

» *Understand your innovation anatomy with InnoSurvey®*

The answer can seem discouragingly elusive, but the underlying truth is that each organization contains its own individual seeds of success or failure. Repeatable success depends on leaders nurturing the right combination of elements with exquisite precision.

Penker and his team studied more than 1,000 companies across 62 countries to build the world's largest innovation database, the InnoSurvey®. This contains a compilation of insights from multiple respondents for each company, including both external and internal stakeholders, that yields a comprehensive 360-degree analysis of what, why, and how innovation projects came to fruition.

Over the years, the team has been able to refine and develop these specialized methods for anatomizing innovation. This approach provides an iterative, evidence-based assessment that serves as the road map for future investments.

» *The Overarching Goal of this book series*

The goal for the five volumes of this book series is to help more great ideas find practical expression and help more companies survive despite market upheavals.

The five volumes cover:

1. How to Assess and Measure Business Innovation
2. The Elements of Innovation
3. A Complete Innovation System from Ideation to Governance
4. Tactical Innovation Techniques in Practice

5. Sustainable Growth and Profits: Managing Your Innovation Strategy, Organization, and Initiatives

Even when the business environment is changing with blinding speed and large-scale cultural shifts are resetting the market's priorities in unpredictable ways, there's no reason to throw up your hands if you are a business leader. This book series is meant to be a firm grounding you can return to again and again. There are many precedents within the InnoSurvey to help you make sense of what's happening with each innovation you introduce.

What the world has in store for the years ahead is likely to be radically, shockingly new, but you can prepare yourself and your organization to soar above the whirlwind. This book series offers a repeatable, teachable process to innovate for sustainable growth. i.e. greater market shares, and profits—no matter how the world changes.

CHAPTER 2
INTRODUCTION TO VOLUME 5: SUSTAINABLE GROWTH AND PROFITS

Innovations are infinite, even within a finite market. However, not all innovations start with the same chance at a fully productive lifecycle. Innovations that survive are most often those that are supported by an organizational culture that plans innovation strategically and maintains a portfolio of ideas that function well in relation to each other.

From my earliest days, I was struck by the riddle of why some companies become cultural fixtures while others seem to flare out or just fade away. The answer has eluded many investigators who have pursued it with all their considerable might.

The Innovation360 Group was built to boost the odds in favor of the innovators. The first weapon in their arsenal is the Innovation Assessment InnoSurvey, a customized report with extensive, detailed recommendations on what a company needs to do to provide optimal support for successful innovation.

» *The Key to Successful Innovation*

Every organization innovates in its own unique way, and each holds the key to its own success. That key is related to how the organization chooses to execute new ideas. A sustainable, repeatable process derives from eliminating chance wherever possible and making maximal use of the organization's defining strengths.

The InnoSurvey crystallizes the collective experience of more than 1,000 organizations and countless creative projects across 62 countries into the world's largest innovation database.

The centerpiece of the knowledge that emerges from the InnoSurvey is a data visualization called the Wheel of Innovation, which plots specific company

21

strengths and weaknesses onto a map of success factors. The Wheel of Innovation visualizes innovation capability measurements by means of 16 aspects, organizing 66 core capabilities that drive successful innovation.

Over the years, the Innovation360 team has refined and developed specialized methods for anatomizing innovation. The resulting approach provides an iterative, evidence-based assessment that any organization can use bot as the road map for and to manage their portfolio of investments in future innovation projects.

This is critical, because innovations rarely survive on their own. The substrate must be an organization that has codified its innovation strategy, a system for easily managing repeatable innovation processes, and a portfolio of innovation investments that work together for a more substantial market impact.

This is a fundamental necessity for innovation projects in order to perform and deliver value in both the first, second, and third time horizons of for sustainable growth and profits.

» *Successful Innovation Strategies Span Over Three Time Horizons*

As a refresher, let's first have a look at the three horizons, H1, H2 and H3, first defined by M. Baghai, S. Coley, and D. White (1999), as they are used in this book series.

Innovation projects can be assigned to three time horizons that each evolve along a predictable S-curve.

The first horizon (H1) concerns smaller, incremental innovations that build on existing business models, extending the existing S-curve of the company's products, services, internal systems and processes. These innovation projects are common because they require little to no structural change or lead time.

The second horizon (H2) is more creative and proactive, expanding and building new business models, solutions, and internal system and processes, sometimes even into new verticals.

The third horizon (H3) is sometimes characterized as "moon shots" or "skunk works." This is a much more explorative approach to find future S-curves that could be commercialized in H2, and when successful, often ending up in delivering significant cash flows in H1.

Ideally, an organization should be working on all three horizons simultaneously; using an innovation portfolio as its management tool that details how they all work together.

The biggest failure of many contemporary organizations and their innovation strategies is that they are stuck on H1. Some studies indicate that up to 99 percent of businesses are trapped there due to what we call a "spiral staircase" leadership style.[1] That is, in the interest of their own safety and due to their aversion to risk, leaders mandate short-term projects with narrowly-defined goals and predictable ROI. This is not a strategy that supports sustainable growth and profits!

» *Data That Provides Background and Support for Successful Innovation*

Here is some statistical background and support for the discussion, based on analysis of data from the thousands of organizations in the InnoSurvey database:

- 78% state that their organizations are making substantial efforts to innovate.

- 81% of the enterprises say they innovate to grow their market while a slightly smaller percentage, 74%, say that they innovate to increase their profit.

- The organizations stating they drive growth rather than profit have what we call a dominant "fertile field" leadership style, while those claiming that they drive profit rather than growth use what we call the "spiral staircase" leadership style[2] as their dominant style.

Based on data from more than 1000 thousand organizations in 62 countries in the InnoSurvey database, our Innovation360 practitioners and consultants have worked closely with just over 100 of them. Across these 100 clients, 27 demonstrated double-digit year-to-year growth over at least three years. These 27 organizations share the following characteristics:

1. DNA Focus: People within the organization regularly discuss and analyze

---

[1] A style where the organization tries to use existing capabilities and resources in a new way (defined by Loewe, Williamson, & Wood, 2001).

[2] A style where you climb upward without losing the overall direction toward the goal (defined by Loewe, Williamson, & Wood, 2001).

what employees are really good at and what differentiates its customer value proposition, which extends far beyond traditional customer specifications and evaluations. There are many famous and successful companies in this category, ranging from IBM to Google, Volvo and 3M.

2. Real Need Focus: The organization tries to satisfy its customers' real needs, not the needs identified by customers in response to direct questions. The best-known example is Apple—time after time, Apple has launched superior products based on real needs rather than apparent market and customer requirements. The same is true for many famous luxury brands.

3. Reinforcing the Value Proposition: The organization strives to consistently reinforce what they really offer the market, keeping their market position and brand perception intact, while at the same time driving innovation in all aspects of their business from products to business model. One example is BMW's consistently reinforced slogan, "The Ultimate Driving Machine."

4. Technology-Driven Strategy: The organization follows the directions suggested by its technological capabilities, leveraging its investments in research and development to drive breakthrough innovation and incremental change, and seeking to solve the unarticulated needs of its customers. One example is Ericsson and its leading technologies for mobile systems, 3G, 4G and now 5G.

» *Correlation, Not Causation, Reveals the Truth Behind Successful Innovation*

One important takeaway is that innovation seems to be more tightly correlated to growth than profit, simply because profit can be generated or eroded by external factors and good or bad judgment.

However, even if we can see some correlation between strong innovation capabilities and growth, and that more of our respondents state they drive innovation for market growth rather than short-term profit, we must remain cautious about confusing correlation with causation. In our research we see that growth is correlated to innovation, which causes profit, but profit is not necessarily correlated to innovation.

Many industry analysts and management consultants have tried to discover the magic behind success over the years. One of the most telling examinations is that of Jim Collins, author of *Good to Great*. Collins recently followed up on the companies he identified as great, and the results were discouraging, as reflected in his book title *How the Mighty Fall*. He discovered that 11 of the 60 "great companies" he listed have deteriorated to "mediocrity or worse" in the intervening years.

We have adapted our methods to focus on sustainable growth and profits, not isolated successes. We followed an approach based on the assumption that if we conduct our research on a wide range of organizations, not just industry leaders or the work of experts, we will end up with more practical advice.

» *The 360° Approach Provides a Comprehensive Viewpoint*

Assessing organizations by accumulating insights from a host of respondents with very different perspectives, we end up with a more holistic, comprehensive view of what works for innovation projects in the real world. We call this the 360° approach.

We have made great efforts to include data from as many industries, organizational sizes, and countries as possible. We dig beneath the surface to determine both how organizations are making substantial efforts to innovate and why they do it, so we can better understand the mechanisms that drive successful innovation.

The details on our approach to self-evaluation and metrics for innovation are contained in *Volume 1: How to Assess and Measure Business Innovation*. The technical details of the elements of our InnoSurvey database can be found in *Volume 2: The Elements of Innovation*.

Here, in *Volume 5: Sustainable growth and Profits*, we will dive into the depths of innovation strategy development, leadership and culture to support innovation, external and internal analysis, platform thinking, innovation change management, organizational design for innovation, artificial intelligence (AI) as well as sustainability and ethics.

We will look into original business models and examine how orchestrating networks will help you reinvent yourself and your place in the market iteratively, based on your organizational DNA—what you really good at.

We will also describe how to craft your organization's strategy that is centered around your higher purpose, that organizational DNA, and your sustainable innovation capabilities.

» *Turbulence Provides a Great Upside for Successful Innovators*

One of the benefits of living in turbulent times is the opportunity for successful innovators to secure substantial market gains from all the changes, even as established and conservative enterprises lose their hold on their markets.

One example of today's turbulence is artificial intelligence, or AI. AI is already influencing concepts related to business models, internal efficiency, and utterly new ideas about the function of services and products. AI is a powerful engine for innovation and will continue to be so in the years ahead. Yet not enough has been written on this vital topic, apart from dire warnings and dystopian or opportunistic prophecies.

A recent report by the US Executive Office of the President (2016) suggests that the largest negative effect of AI and workplace automation will be seen in the elimination of lower-wage jobs. There is plenty of evidence that it will also reshape the responsibilities of higher-wage fields like legal, medical, and consulting as well. There is a strong risk that AI and automation will increase the wage gap between less-educated and more-educated workers and increase the gap in economic inequality.

Governments, academic circles, and organizations can make decisions right now about what role they intend to play in the future application of AI through research and innovation. At the same time, they have a collective responsibility to channel shared resources to the growth of a skilled, diverse workforce that can thrive in the coming AI-augmented world.

We, at innovation360, have also made decisions about AI, as we have built and implemented "Sherlock", an AI application, into our innovation database InnoSurvey in order to master innovation assessment and analysis and provide extremely sharp evidence-based recommendations for innovation capability improvement to its users.

AI needs to be understood by C-levels, even if it is deep tech, simply because otherwise they will make the wrong decisions. This is why we have devoted a full chapter, on a rather deep level, to AI and how it really works in this volume of our book series.

To conclude, the key message that we want to deliver across this entire book series is this:

Build on your existing strengths, to compensate for your weaknesses. Innovate for the future, not just for now, and don't charge ahead based on the strength of the idea alone. Successful innovators don't try to be world champion in areas they know they are not good at yet. Assess, understand, and act on your capabilities, competencies, leadership styles, culture, and strategy for the three horizons. That is the best way forward if you want to exploit the upside of these turbulent times as a successful Innovator.

CHAPTER 3
THE CHANGING ROLE OF STRATEGY

3.1   Innovation Strategies

Innovation is commonly defined as the introduction of new technologies (*Encyclopedia Britannica*, 1974), and is held by some writers to be a primary factor in economic growth. This notion forms the core of the interpretation used in this volume and the whole series. Innovations are driven by opportunities and capabilities. In particular, Peter Drucker (1998) identified four areas of opportunity where innovation possibilities occur: unexpected occurrences, contradictions, process needs, and industry and market changes.

There are three additional sources of opportunity external to a given organization: demographic changes, changes in perception, and new knowledge. It is also possible to consider linkage to another organization or organizations as an asset in itself. Tovstiga and Birchall (2005) argue that firms are nodes in larger networks that create value by transforming opportunities into business through the strategic deployment of capabilities. Moreover, they argue that firms are constantly looking for opportunities within the environment to turn a competitive advantage through transformation innovation, ultimately gaining profitable growth.

To summarize, innovation can be seen from two perspectives: from the internal perspective of an organizations capabilities and from the perspective of the external market, where performance can be measured, and success judged (Tovstiga & Birchall, 2005).

As discussed in the introduction, one important takeaway is that innovation seems to be more tightly correlated to growth than profit, simply because profit can be generated or eroded by external factors and good or bad judgment, while growth is a result of the organization's constant attempt to turn opportunities into value, often joint value, for the stakeholders (e.g., customers, clients, partners, employees, contractors, suppliers, management, shareholders, and society as a whole).

At the same time, net profit is essential, even if it is not easy to link it to innovation as such, although it can sometimes be linked to gross margins and operational cost. As the first and second volume of this series describe in detail, innovation can be linked to sales innovation, offer innovation, market innovation, or organizational innovation, as shown in the Wheel of Innovation in figure 1. Market innovation and organizational innovation are based on internal development of capabilities, and are used to develop and amplify the market, consisting of a net of value-creating organizations, as well as creating internal efficiency and cost reductions. Offer innovation and Sales innovation are on the other hand, based on externally oriented capability development, involving offer development (of both products and services) and sales methods, including new ways of understanding unmet market needs.

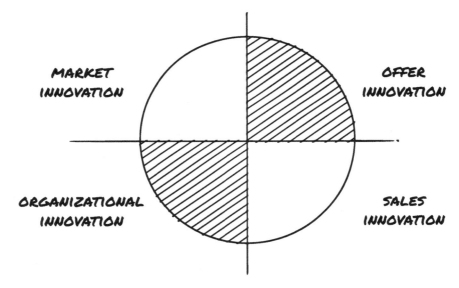

Figure 1: The Wheel of Innovation and its four core quadrants. These concepts are explored further in Volumes 1 and 2.

Depending on the kind of innovation strategy they adopt, organizations can be categorized into three types: need seekers, market readers, and technology drivers. *Need seekers* look for potential opportunities by applying superior understanding of the market and rapid go-to-market initiatives; *market readers* capitalize on existing trends and their understanding of markets; and *technology drivers* strive for breakthrough innovations based on new technology (Jaruzelski & Dehoff, 2010). Recent research, based on more than ten years of measurement, shows that need-seeking organizations that have aligned their strategies with their capabilities are the most successful in generating return on investment in research and development (Jaruzelski, Staack, & Goehle, 2014). At the same time, Innovation360 Group's research indicates that the fastest growing organizations are the ones using technology to create a market advantage. It is logical that need aligned with the right organizational capabilities leads to a higher return on R&D, because there will be a demand for the commercialized innovations; it is also logical that companies using technology to innovate may grow faster, because technology can enable higher degrees of scalability.

Moreover, innovation strategies can also be classified as incremental (improve-ments) or radical (fundamental). According to Penker (2016), there are strong indications that radical innovators (organizations applying radical innovation strategies rather than incremental innovation) are more mature when it comes to handling multiple strategies for innovations, as well as multiple leadership styles. That radical innovators should be more mature and well-structured might come as a surprise, but according to our data and anecdotal evidence from clients, radical innovators that say they only apply radical innovations (meaning that they never apply incremental innovations) are far more structured and goal oriented than e.g. market readers, who apply an incremental innovation strategy reactively rather than proactively. However, our data finds that even companies that state that they do not apply incremental innovation, rather only radical innovation, are fully capable of doing it: they simply choose to apply radical innovation instead.

With the fast-changing, hypercompetitive markets of today, it is not possible to maintain sustainable growth and profits from a stand-alone incremental innovation strategy or five-year strategic plans based on market data that was already outdated when it was first analyzed. What is required today, and that we will elaborate on further down in this chapter, is a full three horizon innovation strategy based on a balanced portfolio of both incremental and radical innovation initiatives.

3.2   Change is the New Constant for innovation strategies

With more connectivity, a growing population, exponential technology development, market dynamics are more volatile and rapidly changing than ever before. What seem to be more stable are the value systems, capabilities, and aspirations within organizations. Value creation takes place within networks of organizations and is limited only by their value systems, capabilities, and aspiration to interact. With increasingly scarce energy, water, health, food and global heating resources, new global values systems are forming new rules of engagement, where social responsibility and sustainability are joining growth and profitability as key components. Sustainable profitable growth calls for both incremental and radical innovation: radical for finding out how to solve the grand challenges we face and incremental for keeping up with day-to-day business.

From a system theory perspective, it is imperative to understand that we are a part of a network of interacting organizations and individuals, constrained by global key drivers and motivated by purpose. The interaction and the strategy for interaction will be covered in this chapter, while leadership and culture will be covered in chapter 4.

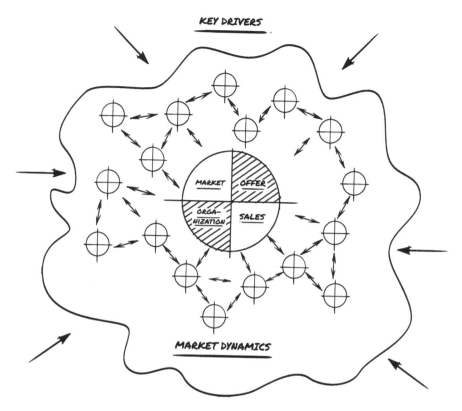

Figure 2: The interaction of an organization with its surrounding ecosystem in creating value by interaction through its capabilities and ability to grow the market, and its approach to organizing its resources and selling/offering to the market. This illustration also shows the impact of global key drivers on the market.

Figure 2 illustrates the impact of global key drivers, such as political, economic, social, technological, legal, environmental and demographical drivers, on the market and how the market creates an interactive dynamic among the organizations in the market. Markets also interact with other markets, and it could be argued that traditional vertical thinking is no longer valuable: instead, the value lies in these key global drivers and the quality of interactions among organizations. Certainly, from an analytical perspective, things must sometimes be simplified, but trades and verticals are most likely not the best way to do it anymore. Rather, by applying the alternative analytical framework of Tuckman (1965, 1977), we may better understand how clusters of organizations (or "ecosystems") are "forming, storming, norming, performing, and potentially adjourning," which is discussed in chapter 8, "Leading Change for Innovation."

Clusters are created based on organizations' aspiration to create something bigger together rather than creating something smaller individually. Trust and value systems as well as collaboration skills are essential to succeeding at turning this aspiration to cluster into value creation that is measurable in the triple bottom lines of social, environmental, and financial success.

To be able to analyze and outline strategies for current and foreseen market development, gaining organizational clarity around the eight questions below is recommended:

1. What is the competitive economic environment in which we must operate?

2. How is it changing?

3. What are our assets (tangible and intangible) and how do we use them to give us an advantage relative to competitors? How is our competitiveness changing?

4. Who are our customers/clients/members today? Who will they be tomorrow? What do they/will they "need"?

5. What is our unique value ("sweet spot")?

6. How do we align our assets, our people, and values systems to deliver on our unique sweet spot?

7. How do we handle shrinking sweet spots and the disruptive sweet spots of competitors, both new and potential?

8. How do we organize for interacting with other organizations to identify new sweet spots and prolong, extend, and preserve existing sweet spots, whether they are our own or a part of a cluster/ecosystem?

Chapter 5, "External Analysis" and chapter 6, "Internal Analysis" will provide a more in-depth discussion of these topics and some of the techniques used for analysis. However, it is important to note that external and internal aspects cannot be fully separated, as they interact with each other on several systemic levels: among markets, between clusters of organizations in the same market, within clusters, between single organizations, and even inside an organization. Think of systemic boundaries as biological membranes, keeping organisms separated but still interacting with the outer world, forming complex systems and sometimes even transferring material—like proteins— among different parts of the system.

3.3   Innovation strategy for Sustainable development

Basically, sustainability is about doing more with less, an idea that most people and organizations across the globe would say is smart, as you can earn more both at present and in the future. Destroying the Earth and consuming all the resources seems to be a less intelligent approach over time; producing with fewer resources today seems to be economically favorable if it is done in the right way. Here lies the rope trick—or should we just call it capabilities for radical innovation? — where new solutions are tested, vetted, and commercialized in both internal and external innovations. The cornerstones of sustainability and circular economy are "reduce, reuse, and recycle," and all of this can be achieved either incrementally or radically. But by doing it radically, we can actually both make a substantial change and gain a favorable market position.

3.4   Linking Innovation Strategy to Imperative External Requirements

There's a new EU directive for 2018 that very well may have a deep impact on the lives of individuals, organizations, and nations well into the future.[3] In essence, the law requires large firms and their subsidiaries to begin reporting on material aspects of their non-financial performance related to environmental, social, and governance (ESG) issues. This new report will include disclosure on progress related to hot button issues like gender equality, the rights of workers, the environmental impact of operations, and compliance with local laws. The goal is to prevent adverse impacts whenever possible and mitigate others as soon as they are discovered. While there's no equivalent reporting requirement for organizations outside EU yet, the directive does apply to some European subsidiaries of non EU organizations. As defined by the EU and member states, public interest entities (PIEs) fall under the jurisdiction of this new directive and will need to declare where they stand on ESG issues as well.

So how can an organization define an innovation strategy to meet these new imperative requirements?

---

3 The EU Sustainability Reporting Directive (Directive 2014/95/EU, an amendment to Directive 2013/34/EU).

Well, innovation is born of constraints. Radically new ideas often only appear after the old ones start to break down. In our research, we've found that innovations are more successful when they are introduced in clusters of organizational units, organizations, or even eco-systems. They need support from a management team dedicated to thinking differently and championing new policies, processes, and products, working in tandem.

Many times, some of the best innovations don't even make it to the market stage because they lack a dedicated leadership team and sufficient resources to develop working prototypes. They fail right on the edge of success.

There is a common oversimplification known as "Culture eats strategy for breakfast," which has been wrongly attributed to Peter Drucker. In the real world, balancing real-time management, strategy, and culture is much more complex than that. We have seen many times over that an innovative culture without strategic leadership can only produce sporadic successes, characterized by a wealth of great ideas that go nowhere. At the same time, even the shrewdest leadership can't execute an intelligent strategy without fully understanding what the organization does best. Misalignment of capabilities, culture, and strategy has resulted in some very bad outcomes, both for individual organizations and for the global environment.

Organizations that have failed to live up to commonly accepted ESG standards have typically acted not out of malice but out of expediency. They sought the most direct route to the achievement of financial or productivity goals without sufficient consideration of the impact of their initiatives on others. Those same impulses can be harnessed by a culture of innovation to produce a more empowered workforce that implements better solutions using more sustainable business practices.

In a culture of sustainability, innovative thinking seems to seek the most direct route to a specified goal, but factors in the elements of corporate social responsibility at the earliest stages. Although all sorts of ideas are welcomed and encouraged at the ideation stage, what matters most is a rational decision-making design that selects only the ideas that are best on a variety of criteria, including sustainability.

Plans can change, but planning means everything. It will certainly take time for large enterprises to collect the data, retrain their teams, and generate sustainability reports for all ESG concerns. Organizations everywhere can take advantage of a substantial advantage in terms of brand reputation and investor recognition by putting a sustainability plan into place now.

Most importantly, businesses outside EU can take the EU sustainability directive as a template for ranking organizations on ethical terms. This framework can identify the scope of an organization's commitment to leadership on ESG issues, and then put pressure on low-ranking firms to review and address their service gaps through innovation.

The new directive is an effective reminder that the public sector does not have a monopoly on enforcing ethical behavior. The commercial sector actually has a greater potential to reshape the world in a more positive light by combining the economic might of large enterprises with the innate human drive to streamline workflows. To quote Johan Roos (2017) 'Practical wisdom strikes balances between individual and common interests, short-term and long-term perspectives as well as between adapting to and shaping the environment'.

In the following section we will dig further into paradoxes and uncertainty and how to handle new regulations, through the necessary and even inspiring limitations of scarce resources, hyper-competition, and call for sustainability.

3.5   Strategies for the Unknown

Kotler and Armstrong (2012) define strategic planning as "the process of developing and maintaining a strategic fit between the organization's goals and capabilities and its changing marketing opportunities." Planning involves adapting to take advantage of opportunities in the organization's constantly changing environment (Kotler & Armstrong, 2012). It is clear that the degree of uncertainty, complexity, capability of foreseeing, and half-life of competence are all dramatically curtailed, while demand and supply are increasingly taking off with scarce resources; the result is the traditional strategist's worst nightmare. As we said, five-year plans and huge market surveys are things of the past: today it is all about direction and agility, particularly the agility to change, learn, adapt, overcome, and collaborate within value nets. It is essential to acquire, develop, and utilize our capabilities for innovation in a strategic direction and within a context of an ecosystem where value is created such that barriers to entry are increased, fewer resources are needed, and instability becomes a temporary equilibrium (until the next seismic shift). In a nutshell, this is how we can handle uncertainty, turning from denial to acceptance.

According to Penker (2016, 2017), companies and organizations—consciously or unconsciously—develop strategies, leadership, culture, capabilities, and competencies that they use to improve and innovate their business, both internally (e.g., processes) and externally (e.g., value proposition).

McKinsey's Steve Coley uses the three horizons briefly described in Chapter 2 to represent parallel innovation activities in terms of overlapping S-curves. We will elaborate these concepts further here as they are very important for defining a balanced innovation strategy for sustainable growth and profits:

- **Horizon 1** (H1) refers to incremental innovation in the current business. Incremental innovation extends the existing S-curve of an organization.

- **Horizon 2** (H2) is about expanding and building new businesses based on more radical innovation, thus forming the company's next S-curve.

- **Horizon 3** (H3) is an explorative approach based on radical innovation to identifying and testing future possible S-curves, to be commercialized in H2, and ultimately ending in H1.

O'Reilly and Tushman (2004) propose the latent possibility of working ambidextrously[4] with both incremental and radical innovation. Dividing innovation work into different "horizons" in order to manage it effectively is common knowledge in the business world, particularly among C-level executives. Despite this, however, many companies still prioritize large H1 projects, and the result is numerous projects that frequently create less value for the company than H2 or H3 projects would.

To counteract this trend, companies could use their common resources optimally to improve and protect their current profit (H1), while simultaneously developing tomorrow's earnings and market share (H2) and learning for the future (H3). This would involve using and developing their leadership, culture, capabilities, and competencies most efficiently and, as advised by Scott, killing the "zombie

---

4 According to O'Reilly and Tushman (2004), the ability to simultaneously pursue both incremental and discontinuous innovation, from hosting multiple contradictory structures, processes, to cultures within the same firm.

projects" in H1—those projects that "fail to fulfill their promise and yet keep sucking up resources" (Scott, Duncan, & Siren, 2015). To achieve this, companies need to understand how to organize and transform themselves into organizations that are able to work in the short, medium, and long term, while maximizing their use of both tangible and intangible resources.

A successful innovation strategy for the unknown is therefore based on the fact that the three horizons call for different strategies, leadership styles, capabilities, competencies, and metrics, as indicated by the correlations in the data studied by Penker (2016) and shown in Table 1. [5]

	Horizon 1	**Horizon 2**	**Horizon 3**
Scope **Strategic focus**	Core business Exploit and optimize existing business— incremental innovation	Growth business Expand existing business while simultaneously building new business	Future business Explore options, place small bets on emerging opportunities (radical innovation)
Innovation strategy	Market reader, technology drivers (incremental)	Technology drivers (partly radical) and need seekers	Technology drivers (radical) and need seekers
Leadership style	Spiral Staircase	Cauldron, Fertile Field, Pac-Man	Explorer
Capabilities with a strong correlation to strategy and leadership	Clear vision, goal-oriented leadership, core focus, market insights	Platform and design thinking, prototyping, speed to market, project selection, ideation	External knowledge sharing, co-creation, open innovation, anthropology, technology watch
Competencies	Fully assembled	To be acquired or developed	Requirements uncertain
Metrics	Return on investment	To be acquired or developed Net present value based on prototyping and hypothesis	Requirements uncertain Strategic option value based on scenarios

Table 1: Horizon characteristics. Based on work between 2008 and 2016 by Penker, Ohr, and McFarthing (2013), Jaruzelski and Dehoff (2010), and Loewe, Williamson, and Wood (2001). All data are collected and analyzed in InnoSurvey (2016).

---

5 Data structure in the InnoSurvey is based on the Innovation360 Framework and is divided into the categories of Why (strategy), What (type of innovation), and How (66 capabilities, 4 process steps, and 10 personas).

Horizon 1. Most companies put as much as 99 percent of their core efforts into H1, using the incremental/spiral staircase leadership style described earlier. Leaders work step by step toward well-defined goals, calculating ROI and predicting the future. Capabilities that are typically important for Horizon 1 include having a clear vision, having goal-oriented leadership, coaching around goal setting, focusing and building on the core of the organization, and gaining insights into the market.

Horizon 2. This strategy is based on anticipating market needs and using technology in new ways, instead of reading the market and responding to it. Crucial capabilities are platform and design thinking, user research, prototyping, ideation, project selection, and speed. The H2 leadership styles are entrepreneurial: challenging the business model, also called Cauldron style[6] ; seed-funding external innovation projects and then buying them back, also called Pac-Man[7] ; and acting as the gardener, keeping what works while removing what does not, also called Fertile Field. H2 projects are measurable to the extent that managers work with small experiments and prototypes in order to build the base for cash-flow assumptions.

Horizon 3 is explorative in style, investigating needs on a deeper level and using new technologies for disruption. To sharpen future possibilities through external knowledge sharing, open innovation and co-creation become essential. A common management style includes seed-funding external innovation projects and then buying them back, also called Explorer. H3 projects cannot be measured by traditional methods such as ROI; rather, they are about exploration and learning.

Chapter 4, "The Changing Role of Leadership and Culture" provides more information regarding the leadership styles referred to in Table 1.

Analysis of these strategic horizons should be based on both external and internal information, which can include both quantitative and qualitative data. In this type of analytical process, based on the company's strategic direction, external context (opportunities and threats), and internal context (strengths and weaknesses), you can identify what's blocking forward strategic motion and what could be done to amplify it—alone or in the collective efforts that form ecosystems. The resulting understanding of the context and strategic direction forms the basis for solutions

6 An entrepreneurial style where the business model is frequently challenged (defined by Loewe, Williamson, & Wood, 2001).

7 A style where you invent, outsource, and finance start-ups (defined by Loewe, Williamson, & Wood, 2001).

that can:

1. **Remove blockages** that are hindering or slowing down movement in the strategic direction. These are typically misalignments or lack of capabilities needed for a given leadership style or innovation strategy.

2. **Amplify the strategic direction**. One typical approach of this kind is to identify and initiate more innovation projects in the third horizon to support the second and first horizons. To do that, you can engage people in specific places in the organization who have the right leadership and capabilities to execute this approach (identified in your data analysis).

Options should next be outlined based on the external and internal analysis, alignment, benchmarks, correlations, and initial plans for removing blockages and amplifying the strategic direction of the organization. Typically, recommendations are based on one of three approaches:

*   **Best Fit**, meaning they are based on how the current situation looks and what's possible without any major changes. This approach is typically based on current conscious strategy, leadership style, type of innovation, and the capabilities and competences that need to be strengthened.

*   **Best in Class**, which are based on the best companies that have the same strategic intent you aim for. These recommendations focus on the changes needed in strategy, leadership styles, type of innovation, personas (the culture), capabilities, and competences.

*   **Resource-Based View**, which is based on the company's current capabilities, personas, and competencies. This view focuses on what is realistically possible and how that can be aligned with the company's existing overall strategic direction by elaborating on innovation strategy, leadership styles, and type of innovation.

Each of these approaches is discussed in further detail in the following sections.

3.5.1.1 Best Fit

Best Fit is attractive to most organizations because organizations simply do not like change. Best Fit is a way of improving on what is, rather than on what might be. Typically, you benchmark against known competitors and elaborate on what you already have and the direction you are already heading in. The advantage is that it will not take much time and most likely will not lead to any major internal

41

challenges. The weakness, of course, is that it might not help you meet the challenges emerging in your market. Our recommendation is to use this option only as the last alternative, as it often has very little impact and can actually distract the organization from addressing the real challenges in a world that is changing faster than ever.

3.5.1.2 Best in Class

Best in Class is like Best Fit, but you compare yourself with the best organizations with a similar strategic direction, regardless of their geography, customer base, or industry. This is a more ambitious approach than Best Fit and can often be accomplished incrementally and without major disruption to the company; however, it requires that your organization be open to change and that you learn from organizations outside your own industry.

3.5.1.3 Resource-Based View

The Resource-Based View (RBV) builds the competitive advantage of the company primarily through its application of a bundle of valuable tangible or intangible resources. In order to transform a short-term competitive advantage into a sustained competitive advantage, these resources must be aligned with the organization's strategy. In practice RBV has been shown to generate sustainable competitive advances simply because you elaborate on what you are really good at instead of compensating for your weaknesses or trying to imitate something you cannot imitate.

CHAPTER 4

THE CHANGING ROLE
OF LEADERSHIP AND CULTURE

With the current market volatility and fast pace of change, it is hardly surprising that there is a need for revised approaches to strategy and more flexible, multifaceted leadership. Before digging into the implications of a deeper level of leadership and innovation, let's review the five basic leadership styles, shown in Table 2, that were defined by Loewe, Williamson, and Wood (2001) and also covered in the first volume of this book series. (*Volume 1: How to Assess and Measure Business Innovation*).

The Spiral Staircase leadership style is a goal-oriented approach, with quantitative goals often broken down into small sub-goals and even smaller steps (like *sprints* in scrum development). It typically yields a classic performance management culture. Spiral Staircase is highly effective for the known, where the team is competent and has the right capabilities (such as setting and following up on goals, using commonly known methodologies and processes, knowing how to protect intellectual property, and analyzing the market and demand). However, as soon as you do not know, you cannot not easily define quantitative goals, much less slice them up into sub-goals or even smaller next steps. One example from our projects was the R&D officer at a large, well-respected international firm that was going to start up an innovation center for Horizon 2 and 3 projects, who said, "But we cannot develop artificial intelligence: it is too big and we do not even know where to start." This worry captures it all: the firm was stuck in its preference for Spiral Staircase leadership. The CEO now had two options;

Option 1: Let the R&D manager establish the team and pick the projects they felt comfortable with, and simply accept that the team will produce incremental innovations based on known facts, assessable competencies, and the ability to predict and calculate satisfying return-on-investment analyses.

45

The consequences would be fewer mistakes...but no new innovations.

Option 2: Appoint a new, more flexible and experimental R&D manager, or establish two/several R&D centers (so-called satellites: see the chapter on organizational design for more details) with different horizons.

If the organization's incentive programs and preferred leadership at the highest level encourage Spiral Staircase leadership, then incremental improvements will happen, but no innovations for the future will take place, regardless of the number of R&D managers or the number of innovation centers. You must simply believe it is possible to drive innovation in the face of the unknown. One famous Spiral Staircase example is Kodak, which had its best year ever immediately before its bankruptcy (Chapter 11), simply because they were managing and incentivizing on gross profit and did not want to cannibalize on their core market with new radical innovations such as the digital camera.

On the other hand, even if you do believe innovation is possible at the C-level, it is not enough. We have seen in many assignments that C-suites cannot make innovation happen without enrolling the organization. To succeed, you need to find allied managers with the leadership style appropriate for the task. This is also why it is so important to assess and measure the leadership styles of your organization to identify the right managers (see *Volume 1: How to Assess and Measure Business Innovation*). It also means that you will have to accept that you need many types of leaders, so that all three horizons will be covered with respect to leadership programs, the recruitment process, incentive programs, goal-setting, and ultimately defining the purpose of the organization.

In the second horizon, we have found Fertile Field and Cauldron leadership to be most appropriate. The Cauldron leader is a typical entrepreneur who tries things out, often without much thought, but rather using intuition. The Fertile Field leader is more structured, waiting for the results of (many) tests and watching what's happening before deciding on what to pursue. Both the Fertile Field and the Cauldron leader are trying to solve real problems, and often organize themselves and others with labs, workshops, and sometimes even start-ups: that is what we call the Pac-Man leader. The Pac-Man leader funds an external effort and buys it back if it works. Typical Pac-Man companies are Google, Cisco, and Microsoft. However, it is important to point out that none of those market leaders will be able to find new radical innovations, unless it's by a stroke of luck. The Explorer is the leadership style that constantly researches, tries, learns, collaborates with others, and eventually comes up with something worth doing. The Fertile Field or Cauldron leader, then, is typically the perfect manager to take the idea, experiment with it, and eventually succeed. The challenge with all leadership styles other than the Spiral Staircase is that you will fail; in fact, you need to fail, because otherwise you will not learn and come up with the next innovation that revolutionizes the market or your internal operation.

Now, one could argue, we do not want to take any risk with our own or even other people's money (that is, shareholders). But, in fact, the single biggest risk you can take is to do whatever you did in the past, since in the best case that will lead to the same shrinking margins your competitors face and in the worst case, bankruptcy. Finding new ways of internally solving problems, like digitalization, or externally interacting and creating value, has always been the only way to stay on top in the competition; today, with the high pace of change, it's more necessary than ever.

Leadership	Definition
The Cauldron	An entrepreneurial style where the business model is frequently challenged.
The Spiral Staircase	A style where you climb upward without losing sight of the overall goal.
The Fertile Field	A style where the organization tries to use existing capabilities and resources in a new way.
The Pac-Man	A style where you invent, outsource, and finance start-ups.
The Explorer	A style where you explore possibilities and invest time and money in them without demanding short-term profit.

Table 2: Five kinds of leadership (Source: Loewe, Williamson, & Wood, 2001)

This does not mean that you should not optimize, but the other way around. The whole point is to work in all three horizons at the same time, securing short-, mid-, and long-term growth and profitability—what we call sustainable growth and profits. The chapter on external analysis and internal analysis will cover S-curve analysis and discuss simultaneously working in all three horizons in more detail.

4.1   SMEs and Large Organizations

According to Penker (2016) and Innovation360's global innovation management database, small-to-medium-sized enterprises (SMEs), unlike larger companies, clearly state that they are prioritizing innovation. SMEs perceive themselves as excelling in a clearer vision, ideation, and exploration, setting the scene for H2/H3. Larger corporations perceive their strength in reading the market (H1) and selecting the right innovation projects (H2). It's noteworthy that SMEs exhibit several concomitant leadership styles (up to three), while larger corporations tend to be more uniform. Larger corporations tend to have all types of innovation strategies, which is not the case with SMEs. This illuminates why the management of many SMEs can adapt more easily to an innovation horizon model but may struggle strategically (due to their inflexibility). Larger corporations appear to easily change and set strategy (that is, they are more flexible), but struggle with their leadership when trying to work with innovation horizons. Thus, it seems that SMEs and larger corporations can learn from each other. Also, most large corporations are not monoliths: most of them are composed of multiple business units that each have different leadership and strategies. This is why it is wise to investigate an organization carefully, peering into each corner, in order to understand and build on strength rather than just compensating for weaknesses. Building a balanced portfolio, supported by the optimal organizational context, is the key challenge for the C-levels of today and the coming years. More about portfolio management can be found in Chapter 7, Initiatives and Platform Management.

4.2   Many Layers

The flip side of the leadership coin is the experience of the one being led. Leadership is about understanding yourself, your group, and the society that your group and groups are acting within. The more layers of groups you manage, the more demanding it is to understand and lead based on insights about people and how they become an integrated part of society. One could argue, and many do, that it is easier to be on the first level managing a large organization than to have the role of a professional middle manager. That might have been partly true in the past, but not in recent decades or in the present time. Understanding need, the impact of actions, and relationships, and forming a high-performance culture that drives innovations in a systematic way requires more insight and skill than ever. You must be capable of leading with performance measures while at the same time encouraging exploration and experiments without any hard evidence. You must be able to lead a diverse team, or even many diverse teams, in many different ways. This is why purpose and direction have become much more central in strategy work today.

4.3   Leading with Paradoxes

A paradox involves contradictory yet interrelated elements that exist simultaneously and persist over time. The world is full of paradoxes. When it comes to innovation, we have noticed four common paradoxes worth mentioning. Once you know about them, and can identify your organization as being one of them, you can take the appropriate countermeasures to avoid the pitfalls.

4.3.1.1 The Dr Winterkorn Paradox

Being clear about your goals is normally a very good thing; having high expectations is normally a very good thing; and being visionary and challenging is also normally a very good thing. Nevertheless, when you do not align your strategy and goals with present (and future) capabilities, the company will fail, as VW did with its doctored emission testing. It will simply not be possible for the company to reach radical goals with its current capabilities, strategy, and leadership style if they are not aligned. However, in the case of VW, maintaining its leadership style while making some adjustments to its innovation capabilities, some small strategic adjustments, and a clear organizational vision would most likely have turned VW into Tesla's strongest competitor. Instead of going for world dominance through cost cutting and trying to keep its market position by fraudulent air pollution testing, it would probably have been a better idea to build on the organization's capabilities and define a radical vision with the same determination and goal-oriented leadership they used for the easy fix and ultimately one of the worst cases of fraud in the history. One could argue that it would be hard to justify jeopardizing the company's position by experimenting, but experimenting and having an inspiring vision would not have put VW in the position it is in today, where the whole company is in jeopardy and only time will tell how their story ends.

The paradox is that the best radical innovators who are innovating the unknown are goal oriented, but goal-oriented leaders tend not to believe in radical innovation of the unknown.

4.3.1.2 The Too-Big-to-Fail Paradox

Another interesting paradox is that large corporations with vast resources and a skilled, well-educated management team fail to invest in what is to come (or what to create, i.e. a new blue ocean) and concentrate on what is (over time, always the red ocean). When they do invest, they often fail because they do not organize for innovation: they run all new initiatives in the same way.

To summarize, these are some of the most common mistakes made by large corporations:

- Prioritizing large markets over smaller or undeveloped ones
- Allowing competence to become incompetence
- Not managing internal conflicts and legitimacy problems
- Getting stuck in the market's preferences
- Preserving product architectures that creates deadlocks in the organization
- Developing technology but lacking runways for landing it
- Staying stuck with old technology while new technology is changing the structure of their industry
- Doing investment calculations that discriminate against innovation

The list could be made even longer, with notable failures like Kodak, GM, and Nokia, to mention just a few. Imagine if Kodak had purchased Adobe in 1997. It would have cost a fifth of its market cap, and Kodak would most likely have become one of the most successful and valuable companies today. It did not ask itself what it was really good at (its inherited DNA). Instead, it went for the last cent of the existing market, the photo development aftermarket. Indeed, the company was expert in development, but not in the form it thought (or managed for).

Kodak was managed by the known facts and the present incentive systems were linked to gross margins and profit. Kodak illustrates the paradox that they were too big to fail, but not because of their market cap and earlier profitability: because of their inherited DNA of innovating, taking risks, and building for the future.

The paradox is that with resources and smart cash management you can risk being innovative, but you will not because you don't have to.

4.3.1.3 The Uber Uber Alles Paradox

It is indeed amusing that some EU parliamentarians have tried to block Uber

50

instead of realizing that the phenomenon cannot be stopped. It reminds me of a story from my childhood, when the local symphony orchestra went on strike because of the new string machines, which today seems absolutely ridiculous, but was not at the time. What has happened since then is that there has been a revolution. Live music (with an orchestra) is as popular as ever, music is more accessible and cheaper than ever, and the trade turnover is still flat, but there are new players on the scene, such as Apple, Google, Spotify, and Rhapsody. The point is that anyone can be disrupted, and anyone can come back. One thing is for sure: there will be (over time) an "Uber *Uber Alles*" that will beat Uber, but Uber can, if skillfully managed, keep up for a long time.

The paradox is that the one who is disrupting will also be disrupted, if not properly managed. It is not a law of nature that the disruptive companies of today will stay on the top; in fact, it's more often the other way around.

4.3.1.4 The Lean and the Mauser Paradox

Applying lean can be like putting a Mauser gun in a vice: you will miss very precisely all the time. At the same time, lean and other methods are relevant for optimizing existing markets and maximizing the cash flow as long as possible, which very often are prerequisites for being able to afford to invest in what might be. That in turn could define a new market space, built upon the organization's inherited capabilities,

The paradox is that on one hand, applying lean principles might destroy the company due to a lack of market insights, but on the other hand might create the requisite financial support for new initiatives.

4.4   Diverse Teams

When the topic of diversity arises, many C-levels are eager for advice on how to manage millennials, often based on a mix of frustration and curiosity. There are many characteristics attached to the millennial cohort, like an I-can-do-it-myself attitude, unstructured, multi-taskers, adventurers, and work-life balance. What is for sure is that things are developing today more rapidly than ever before, they are more complex, there are more interactions, and it is easier to reach out to the whole world for markets for talent, suppliers, customers, and end-consumers. Most likely many millennials are formed by these external circumstances; a relevant question is, of course, what the next generation will look like and to what extent we must adapt to new generations.

Still, from the perspective of innovation, what is the most important defense when things are getting faster, more complex, and harder to predict, and industries getting disrupted one by one? Many would argue that demographic diversity (e.g., gender, age, or race) is of less interest in the context of innovation management than gathering a team of people who think and act differently. Harvard Business School professor Linda A. Hill (2014) says that "When people think of diversity today, they typically focus on demographic diversity—differences in nationality, culture, ethnicity or race, and gender. But just because people look different doesn't mean they'll have divergent points of view." She continues,

> The diversity innovation thrives on, the conflict of ideas and options it requires, the patience it needs to test and learn from multiple approaches, and the courage it demands to hold options open until possibilities can be integrated in new and creative ways—all these things can make innovative problem solving feel awkward, stressful, and even unnatural. Without leadership, internal forces common to virtually all groups will stifle and discourage innovation, in spite of everyone's rhetoric about how much they want it.

Tomas Chamorro-Premuzic (2017) argues in a *Harvard Business Review* article that

> ...while diverse team composition does seem to confer an advantage when it comes to generating a wider range of original and useful ideas, experimental studies suggest that such benefits disappear once the team is tasked with deciding which ideas to select and implement, presumably because diversity hinders consensus. A meta-analysis of 108 studies and more than 10,000 teams indicated that the creativity gains produced by higher team diversity are disrupted by the inherent social conflict and decision-making deficits that less homogeneous teams create.

However, Hill argues that leaders can overcome the destructive forces created by diversity by creating communities whose members are bound by common purpose, shared values, and mutual rules of engagement, getting more innovation results over time (Hill, 2017).

Our experience, and the experience of many design and innovation agencies, is that diversity in personas is good when it comes to innovation and creativity. Problems today call for intersectional thinking, opposing views to drive the best solution, and the ability to handle the unexpected—skills that a diverse group doesn't necessarily have, so they are typically needed from a leader. At the same time, as both Tomas Chamorro-Premuzic and Linda A. Hill argue, there are conflicts when bringing diversified teams together—which is the core of creativity, but a hurdle for execution.

Besides managing the challenging dynamics of diverse teams, when managing many horizons simultaneously we also have to live with, and take advantage of, paradoxes. All of this calls for a new kind of leadership that involves building, leading, and motivating diverse teams, while driving the process forward. And it's all taking place within a rapidly changing world where the leader's experience, knowledge, and insights about other industries are of the highest importance. Our experience is that a modern leader needs to be able to work within a structured and motivating context, while at the same time being explorative and encouraging. Finally, as an efficient contemporary leader you must also have the capacity and the guts to close down projects and declare them a learning experience. This will never be easy until you and your team have done it many times.

4.5   Leading with Purpose

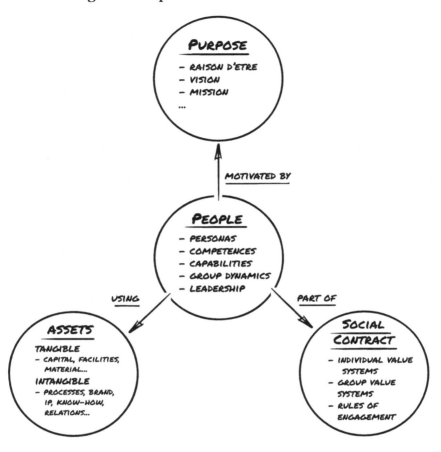

Figure 3: Organizational leadership model (Source: Magnus Penker, based on work between 1997 and 2017)

In recent years a lot of discussion has focused on higher purpose, that is, something great to collectively believe in. In our experience as management consultants, we've found that not all organizations have, or even can have, a higher purpose. We have even seen businesses where the owners do have a higher purpose but the organization does not, and where the owners higher purpose were not even suitable for their current business. Some of these companies have worked indirectly for the alcoholic beverages industry or the tobacco industry, sold telecom subscriptions using aggressive methods, been involved in toxic substances, and so forth. Areas where there can be challenging (or even cynical) to define a higher purpose other than making money. The question is: Should every organization have a higher purpose? Or are just ordinary business goals good enough?

Do you even need a purpose?

Before tackling those questions, let's explore a different perspective. Let's take one of our beloved clients as an example, an entrepreneur selling telecom subscriptions using aggressive methods and reaping a substantial profit over a period of ten years. This entrepreneur used all profits, without exception, to fight for human rights. He took personal risks, he employed people with background that normally prevented them from getting a decent job, and he took care of his employees and their families. Now the question is, what was his higher purpose? Actually, it was to defend what he believed in. Did his personnel share this higher purpose? No, they did not: they were only motivated by short-term sales bonuses. Many of them left his company, started up their own businesses, and competed with him. Eventually, he was driven out of business. It might have been wiser to run the company without this higher purpose and use the profits to promote that purpose elsewhere. It may seem logical to align the owner's will with the business, but it must be possible to align the business logic and the purpose.

The same principle applies to many other professions we have worked with, including media, trading, consulting, and entertainment. On the other hand, a number of organizations with higher purpose have successfully aligned the organization and the owner's will. There are also examples where the owner's will is not linked to the higher purpose, but where the higher purpose motivates the business and generates what the owner expects, typically profit or strategic value. This reasoning shows the complexity of leading with a purpose, and therefore we recommend that you and your organization figures out what you are really good at, why you exist, and what problems you solve (your *raison d'être*), and if possible define your purpose by both formulating both your vision and your mission. However, the most important part is the motivating factor: how can you state a purpose and link that to the organization in such way that all stakeholders, including the owners, are firmly attached to the organization and its purpose and doing their very best to fulfil it every single day? And at the same time accept that people and organizations are very different, and not all people care about high level purposes such as: wanting to solve great challenges and ultimately save the planet? On the other hand, people like entrepreneurs and business owners, often find it necessary to take on lifelong missions to solve important issues in order to motivate them to get out of their beds in the morning.

From our experience, purpose should only be linked to your business when your business is ready or mature enough, and vice versa.

Another important feature of purpose is that it helps support a shared understanding and interpretation of strategy and decision-making, which is especially important when teams with diversified backgrounds need to reach a conclusion when disagreeing. Moreover, as has been pointed out earlier, articulating the value system is essential to gaining the full benefit of having diverse teams with different personas and experience.

In our organizational model, we have identified three levels of social contracts, as illustrated in figure 3. The first is the individual value system, where the individual judges what is right and what is wrong. This system is linked to the second level, the group value system. A group is more complex than the individual, as there might be contradictory values that cannot possibly exist simultaneously. Thus it is essential to express them explicitly, discuss them explicitly, and agree to them explicitly. And as one group is normally part of a larger group and co-exist in parallel within other groups within the larger group, all groups need to agree. Clearly, gaining this agreement has to be an organic process, but it must be curated to be efficient. However, in almost any case it will be impossible to simply state a value system without undertaking a systematic value identification and agreement process. Moreover, it might not be possible for all employees, managers, or external stakeholders to be part of the groups value system and therefore some may need to be handled separately. There is a range of possibilities for accomplishing this, from reorganization to trade-sell, management buy-outs, letting people off to use external measures such as price mechanisms and discount systems, and even binding code-of-conduct policies.

The third level of the social contract defines the rules of engagement, which can be considered a playbook or behavior contract. Explicitly stating values and how they should be among individuals and groups, both internal and external, is an efficient way of enrolling, motivating, and developing people in a desired direction. One common example of the rules of engagement is a code of conduct, typically specifying diversity and gender policies, labor rights, freedom of speech and religion, social responsibilities, waste management, and so on.

To summarize how you can lead with purpose so far, people within organizations are motivated by purpose, and they act based on social contracts. They have different personas, capabilities, and competences, and interact with each other under the leadership of one or several leaders. One way of describing people, especially as a part of a team working together, is to think of their personas, capabilities, and competences in relation to their social contract and purpose.

We will now elaborate and expand one step further on the most central concepts you need to understand to lead with purpose

4.5.1.1 Understand the difference between Capability and Competence

What is the difference between these seemingly identical terms? The simple answer is that capabilities are seen as generic, while competence is found in more specialized fields. Within the organization, according to Assink (2006), the term *capabilities* emphasizes the key role of strategic management in appropriately adapting, integrating, and reconfiguring organizational skills, resources, and functional competencies to match the requirements of a changing environment.

Often, the term *knowledge* is used to describe what we specifically know, while *competence* is broader and includes cognitive ability (intelligence), motor skills, and artistic abilities. In this book, as in the Innovation360 framework for innovation, we use the two terms in the following way:

We use *capability* to define "the organizational ability of an enterprise to successfully undertake action that is intended to affect its long-term growth and both internal and external development". We use *competence* in a broad sense to define "knowledge that you are able to use on different levels: in the collaborative network, organization, and organizational unit, as well as on an individual and personal level."

As illustrated in Table 1, the *competence* requirements for the first horizon, is often well understood, and a gap analysis can be made on each of the groups and individuals based on their role and responsibility. However, the competence requirements for the second and third horizons are not known. At the same time, the *capability* requirement can be mapped to each of the horizons and thereby also to teams, based on the horizon they should work in. This difference is therefore important to understand when building an organization for successful innovation across all three horizons.

4.5.1.2 Use Personas to build successful innovation organizations

As discussed above, diversity in thought and action creates faster and better innovation results, but only if it is properly curated. According to Kelly and Littman (2005) ten personas are typically needed to drive creativity within an organization.

The idea is to create a climate and culture that stimulate innovation, from the first spark of an idea to the profitable results. One person might provide the team with one or several personas; the important thing is to make sure all profiles are present within an organization to stimulate and support innovation processes.

It is important to point out that no organization has the same set of personas, leadership, capabilities, competences, and aspiration for innovation: according to our data, these attributes are spread across organizations in different ways, even if an organization has the same distribution as many other organizations at a summary level.

For more information about how to assess and understand the nature of your organization, please read Volume 1 of this series, *"How to Assess and Measure Business Innovation"*. For more information on how to design an organization for the different horizons based on the organization's characteristics, like personas, read Chapter 9, "Organizational design".

Kelly and Littman divide the ten personas into three categories: learning personas, organizational personas, and building personas. In the early phases of innovation, learning and organizational personas are more important, while in later stages building personas are required.

Figure 4 shows that organizations applying radical innovation have a greater presence of all personas than average organizations.

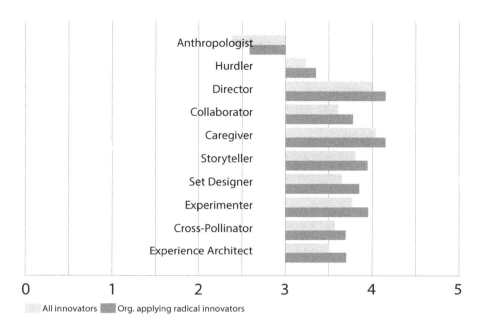

Figure 4: The ten organizational personas (Kelly & Littman, 2005).
Based on data from Innovation360 and InnoSurvey.

Note that the anthropologist persona scores below 3 for both type of organizations, indicating a general lack of anthropologists in all organizations investigated. This is especially alarming if you want to pursue the need seeker strategy for which the anthropologist persona is of instrumental importance.

Mastering the 10 personas is a very powerful tool for you, when you design your own specific innovation organization.

Here is a quick recap on the ten personas. For a full description of the ten personas please refer to Volume 1, *"How to Assess and Measure Business Innovation"*

4.5.1.3 Learning Personas

The *learning personas* are individuals digging for new sources and knowledge. They are typically very useful in the discovery phase, where you look for new possibilities.

The *anthropologist* is a person who ventures into the field to observe how people interact with products, services, and experiences in order to come up with new innovations. He is extremely good at reframing problems in new ways.

The *cross-pollinator* draws associations and connections between seemingly unrelated ideas or concepts in order to break new ground. The cross-pollinator brings big ideas in from the outside world to enliven the organization.

The *experimenter* celebrates the process, not the tools, and tests and retests potential scenarios in order to make ideas tangible. The experimenter invites others to collaborate, while making sure the entire process is saving time and money.

4.5.1.4 Organizational Personas

Organizational personas are the ones structuring, challenging, and orchestrating the work. Typically, these personas are very useful in prototyping and testing, and also in the development phase of innovation.

The *hurdler* is a tireless problem-solver who gets a charge out of tackling things that have never been done before. When confronted with a challenge, the hurdler gracefully sidesteps the obstacle while maintaining a quiet, positive determination.

The *director* has an acute understanding of the bigger picture and a firm grasp on the pulse of the organization. Consequently, the director is talented at setting the stage, targeting opportunities, bringing out the best in the players, and getting things done.

The *collaborator* is the rare person who truly values the team over the individual. The collaborator coaxes people out of their work silos to form multidisciplinary teams. In doing so, he creates opportunities for team members to assume new roles.

4.5.1.5 Building Personas

Building personas are typically the intellectual architects, the storytellers, and the caregivers as well as the ones setting up a proper environment. The building personas are very helpful when it comes to commercialization.

The *experience architect* is a person who relentlessly focuses on creating remarkable individual experiences. This persona facilitates positive encounters through products, services, digital interactions, spaces, or events.

Set designers view every day as a chance to liven up their workspace. The set designer creates work environments that celebrate the individual and stimulate creativity. He also makes adjustments to a physical space to balance private and collaborative work opportunities

The *storyteller* captures our imagination with compelling narratives of initiative, hard work, and innovation. The storyteller can spark emotion and action, transmit values and objectives, foster collaboration, create heroes, and lead people and organizations into the future.

The *caregiver* is the foundation of human-powered innovation. Through empathy, caregivers work to understand each individual customer and to create a relationship.

4.6   Understanding Social Bias and the Stages of Group Development

As mentioned above, according to Tuckman (1965, 1977) groups start by "forming, storming, norming, performing, and potentially adjourning." What's interesting is that during this group development process, a group of people establishes the social contract, connects to a purpose, and utilizes tangible and intangible assets, as shown in figure 3. This also means that the group converges, and the dynamics of conflicts that move the group forward potentially subside, resulting in reduced team creativity and innovation capability. In this textbook we call this phenomenon social bias. To illustrate how this works, we will use a version of the Pólya urn experiment:

1.   Take four urns (#1 to #4)

2.   Keep Urn #1 empty

3.   Place 1,000 red balls in Urn #2

4.   Place 1,000 yellow balls in Urn #3

5.   Place 1,000 white balls in Urn #4

6.   Add one ball of each color to the empty Urn #1.

7.   Draw one ball randomly from Urn #1, put it back, and add another ball of that color from one of the other urns.

8. Do step 7 approximately 500 times.

After step 8 you will statistically end up with a majority of one color in Urn #1 (we'll leave out the mathematical model). This illustrates what typically happens when you ask people to share their ideas or to come up with new ideas. These could be ideas from social media, polls, voting, a top-list that is shared, trend watching, reports, or even workshops. In the end, everything that involves people becomes biased.

The problem with social bias is that everybody tends to have the same idea or the same set of ideas about the same type of problems, which effectively hinders innovations in Horizon 3 and potentially also in Horizon 2. Why is this a problem, then? Because it will limit your competitive advantage/position, since everybody is doing the same thing. So even if what you come up with is really relevant, it will not have any substantial impact on your competitive position, and at best will only defend what you have in the short- and mid-term, until you experience slowly diminishing margins and eventually bankruptcy. This is why diversity is essential to any organization wanting to compete in the future. Without diversity, groups tend to confirm less competitive ideas and solutions for innovation in the second and third horizons.

So, the question is: Shall we divide up groups that have just started to perform (what the Romans called *divide et impera*, Latin for "divide and rule")? The answer lies in what we mean by "perform," and the context provides the answer to that question.

In the first horizon we want conformity, step-by-step improvements, and as few conflicts as possible. We like to know which competences and capabilities to look for, and therefore we keep groups together that are already effectively working together until they come to the stage denoted by Tuckman (1965, 1977) as "adjourning," when it is time to reorganize.

For Horizons 2 and 3 it is a different game: here, conflict is necessary. Social bias will hinder it, but at the same time social contracts can manage it, preventing personal conflicts from growing out of healthy discussions and different point of views. So, for Horizons 2 and 3 we allow the groups to develop their social contracts and strive to reach the higher purpose in the strategic direction set by the organization, while we remain observant on any social bias that might hinder the group's creativity and innovation work.

An interesting possibility that applies in many of our assignments and is further discussed in chapter 9, "Organizational design" is to decentralize innovation and organizations instead of treating all innovation centers (i.e. organizational units), innovation teams, and innovation activities as a monolith. Having many innovation centers or many innovation teams within an innovation center could prevent social bias, as it is mitigated by outside factors; also, teams will form into different socially biased groups and among them create diversity and creative conflicts.

In an interview with the founder of Sun Microsystems and the Sun Labs innovation center, Scott McNealy, he described some of the lab's success factors: to have many teams, not require any particular return on investment, gather the best people with the right attitude in the field of computer science, and let them do what they wanted. All of the teams had two years to prove their results, and every six months they showcased their findings to the organization, which was able to pick and choose among the projects. If a project was picked, the team was obligated to implement the idea, turning it into an innovation in the following six months. This was a way of creating the freedom needed, counteract social bias in the organization and, over time, enable teams to compete for the best solutions. A number of other famous entrepreneurs, such as Richard Branson, have systematically started companies around diversified teams, and allowed them to compete as the organization evolved. The first one to hit the market won: no room for the second-place imitator.

To summarize our discussion on social bias and the stages of group development, innovation is about disturbing equilibrium, temporarily reaching and maintaining equilibrium, and then challenging the equilibrium again. It involves using forces and counterforces to take new positions through disturbance, reaching stability for a while, then challenging it again. A balanced mixture of purpose creating meaning, a common social contract, diversified teams with the right capabilities and aspirations, and the use of tangible and intangible assets in new ways will, if well curated and incorporated into the organizations culture, enable sustainable growth and profits, and thus secure a market leading position.

CHAPTER 5
EXTERNAL ANALYSIS

Creating an organization that fosters innovation in all three horizons requires C-level leaders to analyze and articulate the company's current position, both internally and externally. While conducting a classic SWOT analysis is a standard starting point for any strategic planning process, analyzing the company's external environment and internal position in light of innovation brings a different purpose and motivation to the table, and may also bring important new insights to light. Thus we will spend some time outlining the approach to these types of analysis when creating an innovation-oriented organization.

In this chapter, three layers of external analysis—global key drivers, market maturity and dynamics, and competition and collaboration—will be discussed in depth. Chapter 6, "Internal Analysis" will then focus on internal analysis and how it relates to the external analysis. Chapter 8, "Leading Change for Innovation" will delineate how to lead change projects, particularly how to implement the changes needed in order to execute a strategy. And finally, Chapter 9, "Organizational design", will discuss the options for designing an organization from the innovation strategy perspective.

No organization is isolated from its surroundings; thus understanding external context, i.e. the global key drivers, is the first step to any kind of analysis. Besides identifying the global key drivers, it is crucial to understand the maturity of the market and the market dynamics that encircle the organization. Furthermore, in recent years the collaborative economy and its accompanying globalization have crafted another force that complements the classical competitive landscape: the collaborative landscape.

We will now take a closer look at these kinds of analysis, step by step.

5.1   Global Key Drivers - The PESTLED Framework

One tool we frequently use in external analysis is called "PESTLED," which considers the Political, Economic, Social, Technological, Legal, Environmental, and Demographic key drivers in the organization's environment. We have used this framework in many assignments and have noticed that it is often misused and misinterpreted as a framework for assessing a specific market or even the organization itself. PESTLED is a powerful framework for understanding the global key drivers that influence current and especially future changes and market dynamics.

A PESTLED analysis is typically undertaken as desk research, but to engage a group in handling future impact, completing it in a workshop can be very efficient. What we have noticed in our consulting engagements is that it can be especially efficient to do a PESTLED on both a global level and a regional level, especially when identifying the legal, political and demographic key drivers.

The global key drivers, or forces, are often easy to identify, but the implications can be much harder to assess. To overcome this hurdle, you need to interact with and involve as many stakeholders as possible, as it calls for creativity and articulation of different options. For example, the same force can have both positive and negative impact, and so we recommended that you mark each force as positive (and why) and/or negative (and why).

In many cases, we recommend scenario planning to elaborate on different possibilities. In this approach, the group will:

1. identify a possible issue linked to the driving force or forces (a maximum of two forces is recommended)

2. lock in a time horizon, e.g., "five years from now"

3. identify the stakeholders involved, their impact, and the impact of the force on them

4. define one or two extreme potential outcomes within the time horizon

5. work backwards to understand possible "plots" or evolving scenarios, and how to use or avoid them to support the organization's position

5.1.1.1 Political forces

Political forces are typically a mix of local government and more global trends such as taxes, trade unions, export and import balance, access to advanced technology, labor laws, and visa regulations. We have often noticed that political forces are easy to detect, but it's harder to understand and foresee their consequences. For instance, the Brexit was possible to foresee with a fairly high degree of probability, but it is virtually impossible to predict its impact. However, not doing the homework is not an option, a typical situation for scenario planning.

5.1.1.2 Economical forces

Economic forces include fiscal rules, transfer policies (in multinational organizations), social security fees, requirements for annual reporting (including sustainability reporting), taxes on services and goods, gross national product growth and decline, inflation or deflation, unemployment, government spending, access to capital, interest rates, and so forth.

The economic forces may have more impact than one think, and they're not always about taxes, but rather interest and inflation driving risk appetite in the financial market. For example, recently the low interest rates in the western world have led to back-sourcing from China to the EU and US, as it has simply become more cost-efficient to buy robots and fully automated factories with low interest (at the moment lower than in China), than to let low-cost labor manufacture products in semi-automated or even non-automated Chinese factories. The interest gap between for instance China or Turkey, and EU or US, for example, has simply made it more favorable to back-source the manufacturing. Interestingly, services will be even easier to move, at hardly any cost, when artificial intelligence makes them much cheaper and, in many cases better than with human involvement. However, these gaps will most likely change, and might become the opposite in coming years.

5.1.1.3 Social forces

Unemployment, habits, taste, buyer and consumption patterns, important aspects in people's lives, influencers, and source criticism are some important examples of social driving forces. Lately criticism of sources has become essential and here we typically see parallel trends, some less critical, others more critical, and organizations using it to their advantage. Social driving forces can change very quickly and have a great impact on people's everyday choices about everything from consumption, voting, and education to where and how they work. For example, there are more freelancers available in many more parts of the world than ever before, some by choice and some as a result of circumstances. In many parts of the world it is simply the best way to get into the market. At the same time, we see more and more experts becoming freelancers or independents, earning more, working more globally, and making their own decisions about their situations. Globalization and technology have completely changed the market for talent, and social factors have responded in kind.

5.1.1.4 Technological forces

The speed of technological development has most likely never been as fast as it is at the present time. There are several reasons for this: globalization, building on already available components, low interest rates bringing more funding for risky projects, and technology breakthroughs such as high-speed microprocessors and computer storage capacity. Artificial intelligence, robots, and wireless high-speed communication will change the planet forever, particularly how we define the employment market. And most likely, we will see technologies changing even more, in ways we can't imagine today. At the same time, it can be argued that creativity, art, and superior customer experiences will not be replaced by technology, at least not in the near future. This has to do with the free will of the human race, something explored further in the chapter about artificial intelligence.

5.1.1.5 Legal forces

As long as there are entrepreneurs, it will always be possible to work around laws. Therefore, it is necessary to understand legal forces, while recognizing that they will not remain static nor always work in your favor. We have seen many cases where it is tempting to lay back and enjoy a monopolistic situation just because the law happens to favor your organization. Current examples are banks, financial institutions, and recruitment and staffing companies. At this writing, energy companies, the automotive industry, mining, agriculture, and public and private transportation are examples of industries that are experiencing disruption. In the past it has been media, entertainment, and manufacturing, to mention just a few. All are examples where legal implications either preserve, allow or enforce change. In combination with technology and globalization, laws on employment, intellectual property, data protection, and solvency ratio—to mention just a few examples— have the power to change industries completely.

Let's take an example: In the 1950s it was not legal to run commercial radio stations in many European countries, which preserved the status quo and effectively hindered development, so entrepreneurs found work arounds by broadcasting from radio transmitters on boats in international waters. Another example from today is that new laws about data protection such as GDPR in the EU can encourage entrepreneurs to find new work arounds by building server farms on international waters or in space. So, laws intended to protect can, in conjunction with technology and driven by an entrepreneur, have the total opposite effect. This is the point of analyzing both positive and negative effects of legal driving forces.

5.1.1.6 Environmental forces

The environment is undergoing dramatic changes; regulations, innovations, and the public attitude is affecting reuse, reduction, and recycling; and life cycle management has become central. However, there are many more aspects of environmental driving forces, including climate change, health, security, and outer space. They are broad and concern everything from the physical world that has an impact on us and they are manifested in the whole movement towards a sustainable world in general. The environmental forces are often linked to demographic aspects, such as population growth, habits, city planning, laws, and bi-lateral, multi-lateral, and international policies, agreements, and regulations. Territorial expansions into the sea and outer space are also of interest.

5.1.1.7 Demographic forces

The demographic aspect of driving forces often has the greatest impact. Think of just spoken language and its impact, together with diversity issues, like religion, habits, preferences, and the many, often contradictory, unwritten cultural laws. Think, also, of general migration, of global virtual teams working together for years without meeting each other face to face, and of scarce resources as new generations in developing countries with rapid population growth pursue the same material standard as the developed world has had for decades. Then think of counterforces, like the movement toward less materialism. There are many forces to consider here. In our experience, the demographic analysis often leads to the largest number of forces and counterforces in the PESTLED analysis. The demographic forces are the most complex of all driving forces, not at a high level, but when broken down into its many components—and they are also often the most powerful of all driving forces in the PESTLED.

5.2   The Maturity of a Market – S-Curve analysis

In this book, we define a market as a cluster of up- and downstream producers and consumers, collaborating and/or competing to grow, and generating profit within one or several geographical/political regions. Generally speaking, a market can be in an early stage, growth stage, maturity stage, or declining stage, reflected in the so-called S-curve shown in figure 5, where the "S" in the diagram is sideways. In many markets, a series of innovations can revitalize and increase the size of the market; we call this reinventing the market. Inventions become successfully commercialized innovations, redrawing the boundary and even redefining the market with new and increased growth as a result. The concept of horizons introduced earlier is one lens for analyzing the possible S-curves in the present, raising S-curves, and possible S-curves in the future.

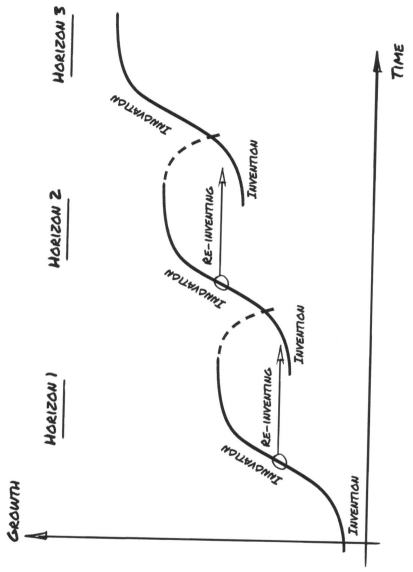

Figure 5: How S-curves, over time, appear, grow, mature, decline, and are replaced by new potential S-curves in future horizons where inventions are turned into innovations and thereby reinvent the market, leading to future growth.

71

5.2.1   Reinventing a Market

Reinvention of a market, where new future innovations expand or redefine the market, means that concepts such as "trade" and "market" can lose their relevance; therefore we use a more general definition of "market" than usual. Having said that, it is still relevant to compete in the first horizon using traditional terms and conditions and using trade and classic market logic. However, it's also important to prepare for the redefinition and reshaping of the market, losing up-trades with cross fertilization and breaking down market barriers.

One example of a market that has been totally reinvented is the music industry. The music industry has undergone an almost metaphysical change, starting as a closed system with limited offerings, produced by a few organizations that controlled both the up- and downstream flow of both recordings and distribution of music through radio, gramophones, and later CD-players. Piracy was a long-debated issue within the industry, and lawsuits hunted people dealing in pirate copies and non-sanctioned live concert recordings. Artists, and especially the music producers, made legal claims when they thought someone was close to violating their intellectual property. Billions were spent on marketing, distribution, and advertising to raise the entrance barriers and increase brand loyalty to artists and producers.

But with the digitalization of the music industry there came a flood of pirate copying, which increased exponentially with streaming. Distributors of streaming music started to produce their own music, and people all over the world followed them by using social media and streaming services such as YouTube. Companies such as Spotify broke all conventions and started to give music away in return for advertising. The entire market was disrupted and totally reinvented where the power shifted hands, the price went down, ownership of music become subscription-based, the "assortment" and variety increased exponentially, and the market as a whole actually grew (and is still increasing in size). What's also interesting is how the music industry has turned into a sustainable business, with instant global distribution, less waste, reduced transportation, less physical storage, and eventually (hopefully) fewer electronic devices needs to be produced as more devices can be reused.

5.2.2 Expanding and Redefining a Market

Expansion and redefinition of a market is less dramatic, as in the case of the car industry, where electric cars are disrupting the aftermarket, as there is very limited need for service and spare parts. The fuel market is, however, totally disrupted. But the car market itself is actually still growing and has only changed slightly from "platforms for fueled vehicles for fun and transportation" to "platforms for electrical vehicles for fun and potentially collaborative transportation." Now, having said that, it may very well be totally disrupted by radical inventions in the third horizon—only time will tell.

5.3 The Collaborative Landscape - The Six Driving Industry Forces

As discussed, today's market logic is more dynamic than ever, and the shapes of market and trades are getting blurry. The rise of ecosystems and new inventions constantly drives change through dynamics. In the classic model created by Michel E. Porter (Institute for Strategy and Competitiveness, 2017), the five forces recommended for analysis are:

1. Threat of Substitutes: What might replace your offer? Typically linked to innovation.

2. Bargaining Power of Suppliers: How strong are your suppliers, do you have scarce resources, and are you in a weak position? Do your competitors have better positions to negotiate around price and volume?

3. Bargaining Power of Buyers: How strong are your buyers? Are you a sub-contractor that only has a few customers who can set the terms and conditions?

4. Threats of New Entrants: Are there new players, disrupting the industry?

5. Rivalry among Existing Competitors: How is the rivalry? Are there many competitors? Do they drive price wars? How strong are they? On which markets do they operate and spend money?

As discussed, market logic is shifting away from simple head-to-head competition, especially in the second and third horizon, where collaboration is essential. Activities like defining new standards, exploring new technology, testing new methods, collectively challenging existing structures, securing long-term supply, and global coverage are all examples where an ecosystem arises and changes the scene. Clusters of actors form ecosystems, from forming, storming, and norming to performing, and at the end fade away and move into the first horizon with classic head-to-head competition, fighting for gross margins and fixed cost structures by gaining economies of scale. The skilled leader realizes this and manages the organization's portfolios, playing according to—and actually driving—the changing market dynamics.

The flip side of competition is collaboration, which is becoming more and more important with e.g. the global drive towards openness and open innovation. We have therefore introduced collaboration, the counterforce to competition, as a sixth force to Porter's classic Five Forces Model (as illustrated in figure 6 below) to better understand and explore the dynamics of a market when we analyze it.

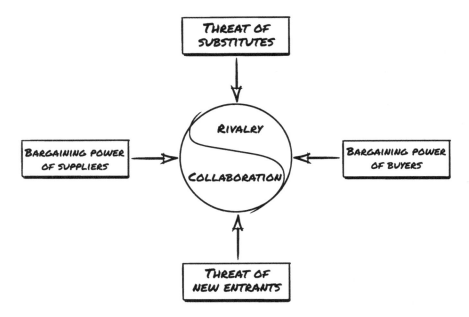

Figure 6: An extended version of Porter's Five Forces, with the sixth force, Collaboration, added.

CHAPTER 6
INTERNAL ANALYSIS

Internal analysis brings the focus to the organization's strengths and weaknesses, and how you use them in the context of the External analysis. This is also the fundamental rationale underlying the Innovation360 approach:

1. Understand the external context:
    a. Key drivers, global and local.
    b. Market maturity and potential disruptions.
    c. The Collaborative landscape and the Six Forces.
2. Investigate and analyze the internal context:
    a. Ongoing business, including organization, assets, access to capital, brand, market, customer relations, intellectual properties, talents, know-how, internal and external portfolio of programs and projects, identified strategic initiatives, and current strategic direction.
    b. Strategic components for driving innovation and change: aspiration, leadership, culture, capabilities, competences.
3. Revise strategic direction based on internal and external context.
4. Identify current valid strategic options, generate new strategic options.
5. Evaluate strategic options based on feasibility and impact. Feasibility is based on the organization's aspiration and ability, while impact is based on the key drivers and market dynamics.
6. Prioritize strategic external and internal initiatives in first, second, and third horizons.
7. Establish a change program to support the strategic change.
8. Work iteratively with step 6 and 7: Managing your portfolio and managing your change programs to keep on top of delivering on the strategic direction.

9. Establish a governance structure for managing and evaluating step 8 (more about this in Chapter 9, Organizational Design).

10. Reassess and secure your organization, constantly improving its aspiration, leadership, culture, capabilities, and competences for innovation and change (material that is covered in detail in the first volume of this series).

Change is the new constant and your organization needs to have the aspiration and the ability to drive change and innovation if it's going to get to and to stay on top of your defined market. Five-year planning and an annual SWOT workshops where the directors lay out the company's direction is no longer working. Start assessing and measuring external and internal context, ironing out strategic options, managing them, while curating and encouraging the aspiration and ability of the organization to deliver today, tomorrow, and the day after that.

6.1   How to Assess Aspiration and Ability for Change and Innovation

Why are some companies more successful than others? Is it coincidence? Do they have a more capable and well-connected board and investors? Is there a super-skilled entrepreneur at the helm? Even more importantly, why do certain companies succeed time after time, while others alternately fail or succeed?

To answer these questions, we first defined a measurement framework and then collected and analyzed data from over 1,000 companies in 62 countries. This undertaking was the basis for the formation of the Innovation360 Group. The subsequent combination of the framework and the databases was named InnoSurvey and was fully commercialized in 2015. Today, they are used by licensed practitioners[8] all over the world.

The Innovation360 Framework (figure 7) is defined by six fundamental questions, often referred to as "the 5 Ws and the H" of problem solving. The framework is based on the conviction that a formal innovation process is necessary in order for a corporation to be a world-class innovator. Based on current thinking, and as discussed earlier in this volume, it stipulates that there can be 5 different leadership styles, 10 different personas, and 66 capabilities (organized within 16 aspects), all supporting the four steps that characterize a well-defined innovation process. Personas, aspects, and innovation process are different perspectives of an

---

8   Licensed practitioners are trained and accredited in the use of the Innovation Framework and InnoSurvey by Innovation360 Group.

organization's capabilities. We consider these perspectives as a way of seeing the innovation through a particular lens (i.e., the personas lens, the aspects lens, and the innovation process lens).

The 66 capabilities, also inherited from current thinking, are organized into 16 innovation aspects, as illustrated in the Wheel of Innovation shown in figure 8. The Wheel of Innovation is inspired by the work of Mohanbir Sawhney, Robert C. Wolcott, and Inigo Arroniz (2006) and is based on the analysis described above, as well as many years of extensive consulting assignments by the authors. The Wheel of Innovation is explored in greater detail in the first and the second volume of this series.

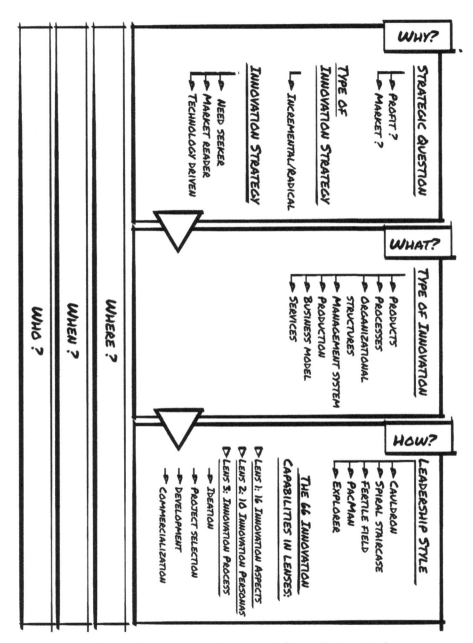

Figure 7: The Innovation360 Framework (Source: Penker, 2011c).

6.2   Why Innovate?

The simple question "Why innovate?" raises deeper questions about the strategic nature and aspiration of innovation. We know innovation is a strategic necessity, because the purpose of innovation is to ensure that your organization survives, and the evidence overwhelmingly shows that any organization that doesn't innovate probably won't stay in business for long. Hence, the innovation process should be aligned with the organization's strategy, and innovation should be a key factor that defines how the strategy will be realized. The relationship between strategy and innovation, and the assumption that they enable and drive each other, is an essential cornerstone of the Innovation360 Framework.

Answering the *why* questions for a specific organization determines, first, whether the organization aims for profit or growth. In the case of NGOs and NPOs, profit can be interpreted as utilization, for example citizen/member advantage or usage. The *why* questions also address the degree to which the organization focuses on small, incremental improvements or radical innovation, or whether the organization is pursuing both at the same time. Finally, the three innovation strategies explored earlier in this volume are also a part of the aspirational *why* questions. Defining *why* for the organization will better help answer the *what, how, where, when,* and *who* questions.

6.3   What to Innovate?

When we ask the second type of aspirational question, "what to innovate," we recognize that the unpredictable nature of change requires us to prepare for many types of innovation options for a wide range of possible futures. Therefore, we use the typology by Trott (2008) to gain greater specificity about the kind of innovation that is applied. The seven types of innovation are:

1. Product Innovation: the development of a new or improved product.

2. Process Innovation: the development of a new process, for instance a manufacturing process, talent-management process, or supply process; typically driven by digitalization, automation, robotics, artificial intelligence, and new man-machine interfaces such as tablets and smartphones that can be integrated into managing and optimizing processes.

3. Organizational Innovation: a new venture division, a new innovation center, internal communication system, and introduction of a new accounting procedure

81

are some examples.

4. Management Innovation: examples include TQM (total quality management) systems, BPR (business processes reengineering), and agile development for software engineering.

5. Production Innovation: quality circles, just-in-time (JIT) manufacturing systems, new production planning software and new, more advanced, technology-related areas such as the Industrial Internet of Things (IIoT), used to connect machines to each other as well as to producers, operators, and even customers.

6. Commercial/Marketing Innovation: can be new financing arrangements, new sales possibilities, pricing models with low-entry process levels, market approaches (e.g., direct marketing); another term is business model innovation, the development of new or improved business models and value propositions.

7. Service Innovation: examples include internet-based financial services (typically referred to as FinTech) and user-experience-based service innovations that use new interfaces like virtual reality and augmented reality.

By linking *why* with *what*, we delineate the strategic aspiration of the innovation-management work within the organization.

6.4   How to Innovate?

The answer to this ability question is universal to all companies, large or small, through the essential mechanism of an innovation process. Whatever it comprises, the process must be driven by strategic intent (the *why* of innovation) so the innovation process itself begins with strategy. The second component of the process is the *what* of innovation; this is a highly strategic question and not just happenstance. Many organizations believe that defining the *what* is one of the first steps, when in fact it takes place in the middle of a strategic, well-implemented innovation process.

In the Innovation Framework, we divide *how* into four components: Leadership Styles, Capabilities, Personas, and the Innovation Process. The leadership styles in the Innovation Framework are based on the previously described work of Loewe, Williamson, and Wood (2001). The innovation personas are based on the Ten Faces of Innovation described in the work of Kelly and Littman. As described earlier, the 66 capabilities in the Innovation Framework are organized into four areas (offer, organizational, sales, and market) and 16 aspects to simplify the analysis. The 16 aspects are briefly discussed here and further explored in Volumes 1 and 2.

6.5   Where to Innovate?

An innovation process is realized through the tools and infrastructure that support it and the people who are involved in the process. Today's innovators need to determine whether their innovation processes will be purely internal or will take some form of open innovation, where stakeholders external to the company or organization are involved in the process. These decisions will determine the innovation infrastructure provided by the company, as well as three related elements:

- The type of innovation (e.g., open innovation, engaging people internally and externally)
- Collaborative platforms to support agile, rapid value creation
- The physical workplace (where people are engaged and motivated)

6.6   When to Innovate?

The simple answer here is "All the time!" However, every activity in a business needs to be assessed to fully understand its impact, and this is especially the case for creative work such as innovation. It is imperative to fully understand what is driving value, and to measure both the work effort and the end results in order to optimize the outcome of the innovation work. In the Innovation Framework, we therefore assume that innovation will take place constantly and at a high pace and that it will be guided and monitored by metrics and coached for value and results.

6.7   The Wheel of Innovation

The Wheel of Innovation is designed to measure the capabilities of an organization. It maps out the 66 capabilities and 16 aspects defined in the Innovation360 Framework. Each of these aspects is discussed in detail in Volume 1 and 2.

In the Wheel of Innovation, each aspect is rated on a scale of 1 to 5:
5 = Changing the Industry (white area)
4 = Strong (white area)
3 = Neutral (between white and gray area)

2 = Weak (gray area)

1 = None (gray area)

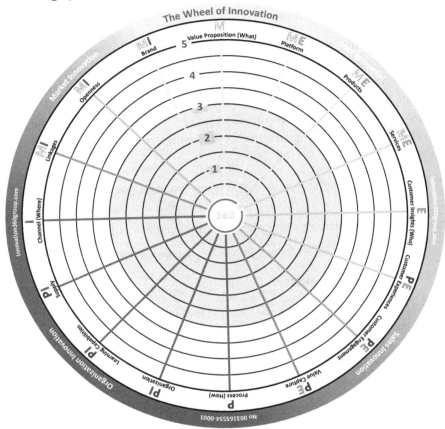

Figure 8: The Wheel of Innovation.

The Wheel of Innovation can be used to plot an organization's profile and compare it to other organizations or industries. In practice, we have found that it is unhelpful to base this profile on the input of one or only a few individuals' perception of the organization's capabilities. In the InnoSurvey database, analysis of the standard deviation for answers to the same questions (related to the capabilities building up the 16 aspects of the Wheel of Innovation) has clearly shown that, regardless of the size, trade, geography, or maturity of the organization, perception matters.

This is the motivation behind the 360-degree approach developed by the authors (2011c), in which many perceptions can be gathered from respondents at many levels of an organization. Over the many years of work and analysis of the companies in the database, the usefulness of measuring the perceptions of external stakeholders, management, and employees has become clearly evident. In practice, a total of 100 respondents has been shown sufficient to provide deep insights into alignments between internal and external stakeholders as well as between management and employees. In large, especially complex organizations, it has also become evident that respondents need to be divided into several subgroups, not simply externals, management, and employees. Data can be collected through interviews, questionnaires, or more advanced digital solutions such as InnoSurvey.

Figure 9: Data from a fast-growing unicorn[9] , based on more than 100 respondents divided into four internal groups and one external group of stakeholders.

9   A unicorn is a start-up company valued at over $1 billion.

Figure 9 illustrates an example of a measurement where InnoSurvey was used to collect data from more than 100 respondents, grouped into four internal groups and one external group. As can be seen in this example, there is considerable variation in the perception of capabilities, but there are also patterns that can be analyzed and assessed, ultimately generating recommendations for the organization. The Wheel of Innovation can also be used for comparison with competitors or other industries, as shown in figure 10.

Figure 10: Data from a fast-growing unicorn (the inner blue line), based on more than 100 respondents, compared with midsized companies in the upper quartile (the outer orange line).

6.7.1.1 The Nomenclature

The Wheel of Innovation is divided into four dimensions (see figure 1):

- Driving External Transformation (E): These capabilities are linked to external transformation, which relates to the offer and to sales.

- Driving Internal Transformation (I): These capabilities are linked to internal

86

transformation, which relates to the organization and marketing. Marketing in this book refers to building capabilities for growing the market, not market activities, which fall under sales. Examples of capabilities for growing the market include reaching out and building great ecosystems, partner channels, and other forms of indirect ways of growing the market.

- Driving Market (M): These capabilities drive market expansion though marketing activities (not the actual sales) and offerings (the product and services).

- Driving Profit (P): These capabilities drive profit by organizational development (efficiency, cost cuts) and sales (the actual sales, how to get paid for the value, engage customers, understand the need and create superior experience).

Each of the 16 aspects in the Wheel of Innovation is described below, in the context of these four dimensions, which will be familiar to those who have read the first and second volume, and are worth repeating.

6.7.1.2 Innovation Aspect: M – Value Proposition (What)

Defining your organization's value proposition is about uncovering what you are really good at—the DNA of the organization—and clearly expressing it, while at the same time attracting the right customers, clients, members, citizens, or other primary target groups. It also requires you to reinforce the offer in every single contact, from lead to sale to aftermarket. The value proposition is essential to driving and expanding the market, and finding the intersection between developing the offer (external context) and building the capability for growing the market (internal context). Typically, entrepreneurial organizations score very high here.

6.7.1.3 Innovation Aspect: M E – Platform

In the first horizon, organizations typically work with incremental innovations, and therefore it is necessary to keep costs and the development timeframe low. By deploying organizational components, blueprints, value offers, and all kinds of documents, including a process description and other useful bits and pieces, it is possible to work with continuous improvements and bring the innovation to market reasonably quickly, while keeping the cost down at the same time. This process is what we call "developing a platform." Typically, it is organized through the use of product life cycle management systems and other software.

The automobile industry is a tangible example where platforms are used to create cost-efficient incremental innovation within the individual organization as well as among organizations creating de facto trade standards.

In the second and the third horizons, platforms focus more on architectural principles, as in the software industry, with its APIs, clean code, and bootstrapping. Technical architectural principles can be used as the inspiration for creating platforms in business, driving reuse, standardization of interfaces to create common ground for fast experiments, and innovation at a fraction of the cost compared with large-scale implementations of organizational changes. Large-scale organizational changes are always risky; therefore, conducting small, fast experiments is an alternative that enables the organization to test an idea before scaling up (although this calls for platform thinking to make it possible).

6.7.1.4 Innovation Aspect: M E – Products

Typically, when we refer to the product development aspect of an organization we mean whether and to what extent there is a systematic and working product development process in place that contains development guidelines, evaluation of competitors' features, and guidelines for planning the market launch. In the Wheel of Innovation, this corresponds only to the development phase of *the innovation process*. The innovation aspect process is broader and contains all innovation process capabilities, while the *services innovation aspect* refers to specific service characteristics. Unlike those two aspects, which are largely internally focused, developing products drives external transformation and market growth.

6.7.1.5 Innovation Aspect: M E – Services

The service aspect encompasses development and evaluation of existing and new services based on the organization's systematic work to gain customer insights. An example of a company doing this successfully is Netflix, which analyzes the kinds of movies customers order, when they do it, and how they do it (for instance, if a viewer who is streaming replays a specific scene). Netflix uses these insights to not only generate services like reminders and recommendations, but also to drive content production. In this way, developing innovative services can cause external transformation that drives market growth. Service design is a discipline that can dramatically improve the productivity and quality of services.

6.7.1.6 Innovation Aspect: E – Customer Insights (Who)

The organization committed to gaining customer insights studies and analyzes customer behavior as well as undertaking frequent independent market research and assessing market potential in order to segment the market in innovative ways. This is typically undertaken by analyzing data from sales, marketing, and customer care, as well as running surveys, interviews, focus groups, and field studies. In this way, the organization generates a deep understanding of customer decision-making processes, which can be used to drive external innovation and the development of internal processes to support it. One famous company generating customer insights based on big data and using it in innovative ways is Amazon, which is creating new data-driven customer offerings from cloud computing and AI to book self-publishing services and logistics.

6.7.1.7 Innovation Aspect: P E – Customer Experience

An organization innovating based on customer experience uses an anthropological approach to studying human behavior in order to gain accurate new customer insights. This data gathering process is typically not pursued though direct interaction but rather through watching and learning. This type of organization builds in automatic evaluations of how customers use and experience innovations, which it can then analyze to determine its next step. It also carries out regular A and B testing of new innovations, systematically comparing customer reactions to variants of the same innovation. Customer experience drives customer loyalty and yields fewer complaints, higher utilization, and ultimately sustainable profit. One of the most well-known firms using this approach is Gillette, which has employed anthropologists to study human behavior and needs on a deeper level. As a result, it has maintained its market position and price level over time, even though its competitors offer similar-quality products at cheaper prices.

6.7.1.8 Innovation Aspect: P E – Customer Engagement

Engaging customers and stakeholders is among the most efficient ways to create sustainable relationships and gain insights on a deeper level than ordinary market research. In this innovation aspect, building a community and involving them through activities such as co-creation, ideation, and rewards is key. Typical industries using this approach are the gaming industry, which encourages mods (modification by users), the software industry, with its open-source communities like Linux, and commercial platforms such as LEGO MINDSTORMS⊠ OS, and Unity, the leading platform for developing computer games. LEGO, Spotify, and several other companies also have open web pages for engagement around innovation (so-called innovation playgrounds), including https://ideas.lego.com and https://community.spotify.com.

6.7.1.9   Innovation Aspect: P E – Value Capture

Capturing and protecting value is essential in the first and some of the second horizons, where commercialization and market penetration are essential. Intellectual property (IP) protection is one component of value capture, but at least as important is claiming a position and visualizing the advantages of being a customer. Proper pricing is important: the organization must develop a pricing system that supports each phase of the offer life cycle, often starting high and decreasing over time. The fashion industry is one of the best examples, where IP protection is secured through trademarks and customer advantages manifested through branding activities such as marketing, product development, retailer and e-shopper involvement, product placement, and customer engagement through, for example, VIP events. The pricing is carefully thought through, starting high and decreasing systematically, until the product ends up in low-price outlets when the season is over. This aspect is highly linked to profit and is concerned mainly with external factors.

6.7.1.10   Innovation Aspect: P – Process (How)

In the context of innovation, the process aspect refers to the complete innovation process—from idea generation, prototyping, a system for project selection, R&D cost control, speed to market, piloting, test methodology, ramp-up mechanism, and risk assessment to analyzing and handling market regulations and management of the complete product life cycle. Typically, the innovation process is linked and adopted depending on the innovation horizon and the company's mix in the innovation portfolio. This aspect is linked strongly to profit and is both internally and externally focused. Examples of successful companies running best-in-class innovation processes are IBM and Google, both of which drive highly efficient innovation portfolios. The gaming industry is far ahead here, as well. However, most companies—even successful ones—lack a culture where learning takes place among the different innovation projects within the different strategic initiatives (and also in different horizons).

6.7.1.11 Innovation Aspect: P I – Organization

Here, the term "organization" is used to describe the company's ability to deliver innovation projects. Capabilities that are especially important to this aspect are engaging and involving people, supporting goal-oriented leadership with a clear vision, and setting a high priority on innovation in all horizons. Idea diffusion within the organization and cross-functional capabilities, together with talent management and reward systems for innovations, are especially important. Well-known examples of best-in-class organizations for this aspect are Procter & Gamble and Fast-Moving Consumer Goods (FMCG). This aspect is internal and typically drives profit.

6.7.1.12 Innovation Aspect: P I – Learning Capabilities

Learning is essential to innovation on several levels. Critical capabilities like being opportunistic, involving C-level management, running cross-disciplinary learning, evaluation, and providing a reward system are essential. Gaining insight from Horizon 3 is especially crucial to succeeding in Horizons 1 and 2. Well-known large corporations operating in all three horizons and rewarded for their learning efforts include IBM, MindTree, and Verizon. In general, learning is an internal activity and is highly linked to profitability.

6.7.1.13 Innovation Aspect: P I – Supply

Supply development concerns scanning and involving suppliers and partners in order to extend the core business that you are really good at. Great examples are e-tailers such as Amazon and Alibaba. Typically, today's organizations go about this by defining new digital solutions, new business models, and new ways of producing and delivering offers to the market through digital trading locations. One interesting example is CellMark, a $3 billion firm operating in 30 countries that has transformed its business model from being a trader itself to acting as a global meeting place for entrepreneurs, and connecting local producers through digital platforms with distributors all over the world. The supply-innovation aspect is internal and strongly linked to profit.

6.7.1.14 Innovation Aspect: I – Channel (Where)

The channel aspect is one of the most important to finding new ways of building the capability to interact with the outside world. It is also one of the hardest to expand and develop, as it is not obvious during a company's emerging phase. Channel development concerns how the offer is consumed, how it is distributed, and its delivery format. For instance, in the gaming industry, the digital platform Steam is the most important channel; in the past, the critical channel was brick-and-mortar game stores. On Steam, game development companies deliver their games electronically and are paid directly by the consumer (a new channel for distribution); the format is new (downloadable and online-connected instead of single-player and based on DVD or DC technology); and it is consumed by adding pre-programmed modifications or by the consumer actually producing personal modifications (so-called "mods"). We can foresee a shift in the channels here, most likely from actors like Apple and Apple TV to new communities with large numbers of users. But to succeed, new channels cannot just add distribution; they also have to find new ways of consuming the products or services, for example by adding machine learning or through new technical formats like VR and AR.

6.7.1.15 Innovation Aspect: M I – Linkages

The linkages aspect is a broad concept that encompasses building and utilizing the so-called ecosystems described in a previous chapter for developing, engaging, and rewarding external parties, benchmarking, reverse-engineering existing solutions, watching and learning about new technology in order to be faster, increasing capacity, and ultimately mitigating risks to keep the speed-to-market rate high. A multifaceted ecosystem is one of the most efficient ways of working in parallel in all three horizons, from incremental innovation to radical technology-driven innovations, even with scarce resources. Linkages increase the size of a company's reachable market and are built upon internal strengths in identifying, collaborating, and exchanging innovations with outside parties.

6.7.1.16 Innovation Aspect: M I – Openness

Openness is not about being uncommercial; it is about setting the stage for creating together, learning together, and eventually protecting IP together through patent exchange. One highly successful project of this kind has been WordPress, the most installed CMS (content management system) in the market, with many third-party products distributed and sold through the platform. Other well-known examples are MySQL and LEGO MINDSTORM, with hundreds of thousands of engineers all over the world contributing to a commercial solution sold to households and schools globally. The openness aspect typically contributes to growth of the market and is based on internal changes and development of capabilities for opening up and sharing.

6.7.1.17 Innovation Aspect: M I – Brand

The aspect "brand" addresses the activities of generating demand, sharing through storytelling, and setting the stage for creating so-called diffusion of new innovations. One industry that was very successful in this aspect in the recent past was the smartphone industry, which was able to generate demand for new products through new standards and ecosystems (like the App Store), by setting the scene (through resellers and operators), and also through storytelling (media, product placement, etc.), quickly getting their new phones and new functions out on a massive global scale. This aspect is also used effectively by the experience industries, such as resorts, movies, gaming, and the music business. It is used for generating and growing the market and is built upon primarily internal activities and capabilities.

6.8 Identifying the Business Model and Strategic Options

Successfully identifying the business model and generating strategic options is the central part of the strategic planning process for any organization. It is based on both the external and internal contexts and the best possible use of the organization's actual and potential strengths in relation to the current and future development of the market and the key drivers that are identified in the first stages of the process.

6.8.1 Understanding the Internal Context

To understand the internal context, there are three things to remember:

1. You must simplify. One way of doing this is to lock in on one or a few perspectives in time, then iterate. Another way is to choose the level of abstraction, try to understand the whole, then tackle the parts. Then iterate.

2. Everything is about perception, and no one can be sure to have the same perception as another person. Articulate your own perception, investigate other people's perceptions, work together, and always remember that your organization is a part of a larger universe, and understanding its perception of your organization is essential.

3. Aspiration and ability are not always aligned, and even if they seem to be, you still need to be careful. Often stakeholders have high aspirations until it comes to a decision or execution, then it might erode. The best approach is to gather the insights, collective ambitions, and abilities of as many stakeholders as possible and determine how they can be aligned.

To summarize, the internal analysis is based upon two rich sources of insight:

1. Collecting, verifying, and understanding

a. Collecting information about the business, including organization, assets, access to capital, brand, market, customer relations, competitors, intellectual properties, talents, know-how, internal and external portfolio of programs and projects, identified strategic initiatives, and current strategic direction.

b. Verifying collected material and gathering examples, such as quotes from interviews or social media, field studies, and workshops.

c. Identifying strategic components for driving innovation and change: aspiration, leadership, culture, capabilities, and competences.

d. Assessing and measuring the strategic components for driving innovation and change.

e. Comparing and contrasting different stakeholders' aspirations.

f. Comparing and contrasting abilities such as leadership, culture, capabilities, and competences and their distribution across the organization

2. Agreeing upon the current state

a. External context (based on the external analysis).

b. Stakeholders' (customers/clients/members, board/owner(s), management, employees) perceptions of the organization.

c. Business model, including cost structures and revenue streams.

d. Aspirations: what's important, what we want, how hard we are willing to work for it.

e. Identified strategic initiatives and potential strategic projects, including progress or status.

One common tool used to describe the business model, current or future, is the Business Model Canvas by Alexander Osterwalder and Yves Pigneur (2010), shown below.

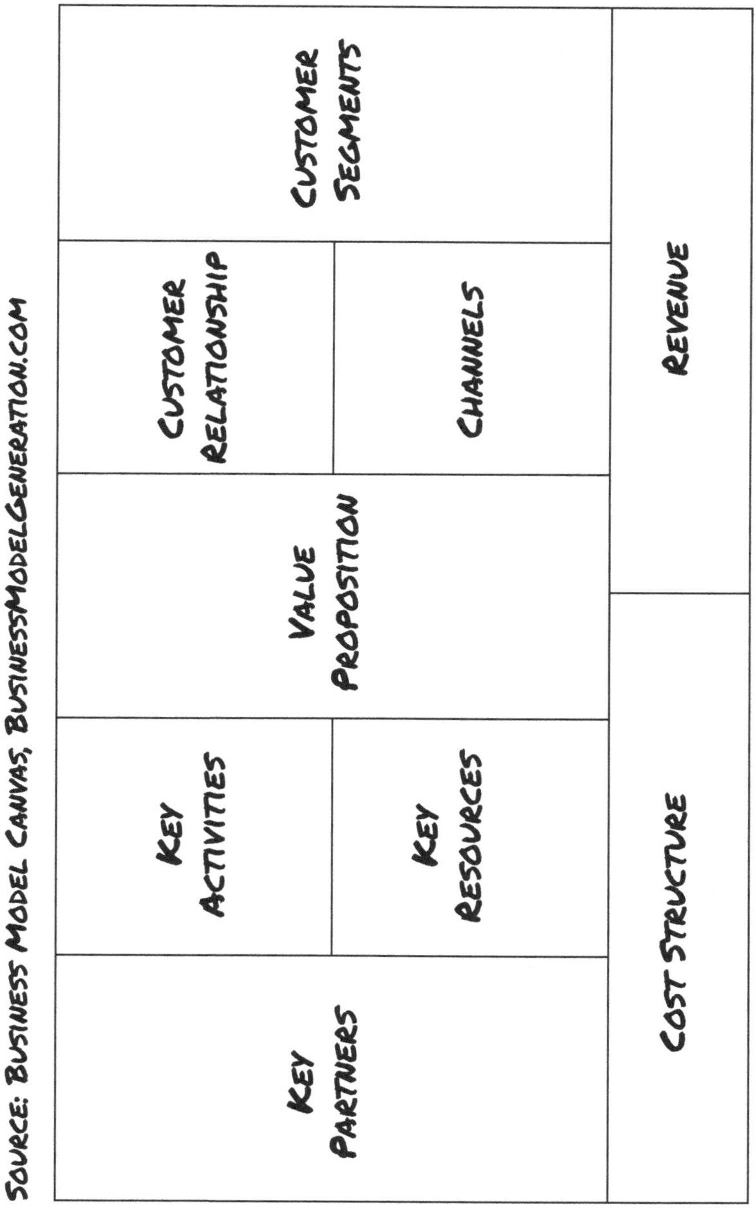

SOURCE: BUSINESS MODEL CANVAS, BUSINESSMODELGENERATION.COM

KEY PARTNERS	KEY ACTIVITIES	VALUE PROPOSITION	CUSTOMER RELATIONSHIP	CUSTOMER SEGMENTS
	KEY RESOURCES		CHANNELS	
COST STRUCTURE			REVENUE	

Figure 11: The Business Model Canvas (Source: Osterwalder & Pigneur, 2010)

95

The Business Model Canvas consists of two parts. The first is internal and describes partners, resources, activities, and the cost structure. The second is external, consisting of channels to the market, customer relationship, and customer segments, as well as revenue streams. The value proposition of the organization is linked to internal and external aspects of the business. Notably, the model posits that executing and developing internal and external parts of an organization require both aspiration and ability—otherwise the development will simply not take place. This is also the reason why it is so important to investigate, analyze, and lead:

a. projects related to internal and external assets and activities themselves, as shown in the Business Model Canvas, and

b. projects related to the aspiration and ability to execute on those projects.

Sometimes it is of interest to dig deeper into operational models, including internal and external reporting structures. However, the disadvantage is that you might very well become totally absorbed by Horizon 1, and go out of business when there are external rapid changes. Our advice, based on experience both leading and consulting with organizations, is to build the capabilities of managing Horizon 1 as an integrated part of the business, and focus strategy on Horizon 2 and 3.

6.8.2   Revise Strategic Direction Based on Internal and External Context

The combination of the external drivers, market structure, and internal context create what we call an outcome space—the hunting ground for innovation and competitive positioning in the short term, midterm, and long term. Here we typically link to competitors' offerings, pricing on the market, gross margins, product and service features, and other related tangible information we have. However, while this is important for Horizon 1, it is not enough for running Horizons 2 and 3. It starts with learnings in Horizon 3 that we can start experimenting with, learn from, and potentially scale up in the second horizon. And as stated before, most of the things done in Horizon 3 will never reach the markets, either internally or externally; still, without them we cannot develop Horizon 2 and will therefore fail when Horizon 1 diminishes and finally fades away. So, revising the innovation strategy must be undertaken by working systematically in Horizon 3 and Horizon

2, and therefore the organization must be able to lead in this way.

The Gordian Knot is to use insights you do not yet have in order to utilize strength you do not yet know you have to do something you do not yet know exists. This is why you must maintain the aspiration to innovate and grow, build the ability to do so, and continuously, step by step, implement what you learn, accepting failure as a sign of success, and when something is working, scaling up very rapidly.

In the fourth volume of this series, we investigate tactics for innovation in the first, second, and third horizons and how you can use that to plan for the strategic work.

6.8.3 Validate Current Strategic Options, and Generate New Ones

It is normally possible to describe future possible states by synthesizing the current agreed-upon state, aspirations, and earlier strategic material.

One way of doing this is to gather stakeholders and ask how they would like to describe the company in the future, perhaps three or five years from now. Then you have a starting point in the current state and a desired future state; you can start challenging from there.

Also, lessons learned from Horizons 2 and 3 will be unevaluable in this stage.

Some may question whether this strategy work could potentially hinder innovation, given its formal process. The answer to this, of course, is no, and that's why we need an innovation system and an organizational design to create it. Innovation should be a continuous process in all organizations, but there needs to be a decision-making mechanism, budgets, and priorities, which are frequently incorporated into strategic planning.

One practical way of ironing out new internal and external strategic initiatives is to model today's business model and the future business model using the Business Model Canvas. Then identify the "delta" between them and ask yourself the following: What do I need to do, internally and externally, to make the future business model come true? The answers will be of two kinds:

1. Projects, or strategic large initiatives, to develop/change specific partners, activities, resources, value propositions (that is, product and service offerings

that solve specific needs), customer relations, channels, customer segments, cost structures, and revenue streams. We call these projects *Business Projects* and categorize them under portfolio management.

2. Projects, or large strategic initiatives, to change the organization's aspiration and abilities. We call these projects *Change Projects* and categorize them as change management programs.

At the end of this activity, compile all strategic initiatives, old and new, describe them, and compare and contrast them to what you collectively agreed upon as a shared future state. If needed, challenge each other again, asking questions like "Is this the aspiration you have?" or "Is this motivating?" or "Is this the best you can do?" or "Is this how you will take the lead and keep on top of things?"

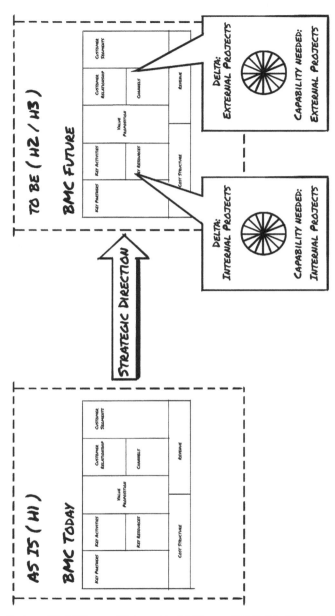

Figure 12: The Business Model Canvas (Osterwalder & Pigneur, 2010). Used for modeling current and future state; the delta is used to identify internal and external projects for change and the ability to change. The Wheel of Innovation's left side represents internal capabilities, while the right side represents external capabilities.

99

6.8.4   Evaluate Strategic Options

When all strategic options—whether broad initiatives or specific projects—are compiled, it is time to link them to feasibility and impact and set priorities.

Feasibility relates to the practical aspects of implementing an option. Do we have the time? The knowledge? The infrastructure, enough capital, and so on? The impact is how much the option will affect growth and profit (for non-profit organizations think usage for members, society, citizens, patients, etc.). By mapping the initiatives to impact and feasibility (see figure 13) it's possible to start prioritizing them as a next step.

Start with initiatives that have high impact and are highly feasible. When doing this, remember that feasibility can be significantly increased by building the right aspiration and abilities, meaning that strategic initiatives can also be linked to change projects. Moreover, strategic initiatives can be linked and dependent on each other, meaning that there might be interlinked strategic initiatives.

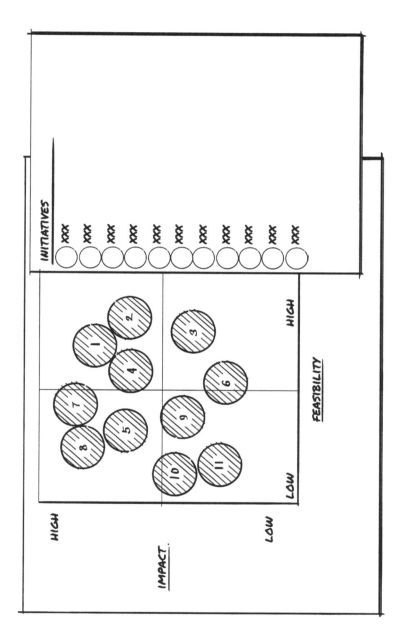

Figure 13: A framework for prioritizing strategic options

6.8.5   Prioritize Strategic External and Internal Initiatives in Each Horizon

When the strategic initiatives are identified and mapped to feasibility and impact, it will be apparent that some business projects are interlinked with change projects, meaning they are dependent on each other and/or reside in different horizons. To simplify, business projects go into portfolio management, while change projects go into change management and overall change programs. It cannot be emphasized enough, however, that both business projects and change projects are essential to the success of executing strategies beyond Horizon 1; therefore they are both also a central part of the strategic planning process. In the section on portfolio management, the process of managing these projects will be further explored.

6.8.5.1 Initiatives in Horizons

One practical way of understanding and planning for strategic initiatives is to map them to horizons, then define the expected results. In the first horizon these results should focus on return on investment, while in the second and third horizons they are about the learnings and insights used for cash flow projects and, if that is not possible, scenario analysis (see Table 1).

6.8.6   Establish a Change Program to Support Strategic Change

Managing change to be able to deliver in all horizons in order to gain and sustain a competitive position is central. It is the basis for Innovation360's methodology, as we have seen that lack of organizational insights and change management are the Achilles heels of implementing and crafting our best possible individual strategy work.

Remember: If everyone has the same strategy, you will all lose—it is just simple game theory. If you build on your present and possible strength, you will be able to set a strategic direction that will be very hard to copy and the entrance barriers will be more favorable to you.

As change management is a central concept, it is explored further in Chapter 8 of this book.

6.9 Linking External and Internal Analysis to Business Development – Using the VMOST Framework

Once the strategic analysis is completed, the VMOST framework described below can be used to express the overall organizational strategy.

Vision Statement: An aspirational description of what the organization would like to achieve or accomplish in the mid- or long-term future. This is intended to serve as a clear guide for choosing current and future courses of action.

Mission Statement: A written declaration of an organization's core purpose and focus that normally remains unchanged over time. Properly crafted mission statements serve as filters to separate what is important from what is not, clearly state which markets will be served and how, and communicate a sense of intended direction to the entire organization. A *mission* is different from a *vision*, in that the mission is the cause. As for the vision, you could say that a given vision serves the organization's mission. An alternative or complement to a mission statement is to define the higher purpose of the organization, based on the core values, preparing all employees, management, customers, and suppliers for what really makes a difference.

Objectives: The measurable result of the actions you take to fulfill the vision in the mid- or long-term future.

Strategic Direction: The approach and direction you take to achieve the objectives. It is important to note that there might be any number of strategies to reach a given objective: that is, there is not one single solution for reaching the objectives that fulfill the vision.

Tactics: The tools you use in pursuing an objective associated with a strategy. Typically, *Tactics* are change programs and identified strategic initiatives (mapped into a project portfolio).

103

CHAPTER 7
STRATEGIC INITIATIVES AND PLATFORM MANAGEMENT

Managing strategic initiatives and platform-based development is imperative to sustainable growth and profits and therefor highlighted in one specific chapter.

7.1   Managing strategic initiatives and Innovation projects

Managing strategic initiatives and innovation projects calls for an efficient innovation process and a working governance model, what we define as an Innovation System (sometimes referred to as: Innovation Management System). Typically, strategic initiatives and innovation projects are generated from work on ideation, where a steering committee (for example, an innovation board) identifies a project leader, and soft and hard resources are allocated, a budget set, and an expected outcome defined.

In the first horizon, the expected outcome is typically return on investment defined by cash flow or even earning level, while in the second horizon it is more about vetting a pilot test; and in the third horizon, it is more about learnings or insights to be used later, in Horizon 2 initiatives.

When dealing with the second and third horizon, projects can very well reach a dead end, where you simply do not know what steps to take. When you face a dead end, or a very high level of uncertainty, generate what we call a spike—a request for another ideation/project selection iteration where you can look at earlier possibilities, generating new possibilities and eventually combining the two. The ideation and project selection phases are elaborated in detail in the fourth volume of this book series.

A generic illustration of an innovation system is shown in figure 14, starting with aspiration and ability, linking to strategy, then gaining insights, and exploring possibilities through experimentation. When experiments are successful, they are typically presented to an innovation board for vetting, and resources and the expected outcome are defined, along with a budget. Typically, an innovation board or other steering committee meets to monitor and prioritize the projects, as projects always compete for common, mostly scarce, resources such as capital, facilities, talent, marketing, test customers, suppliers, and test equipment.

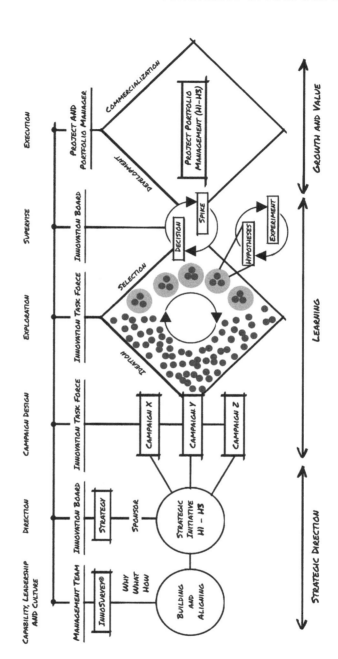

Figure 14: An illustration of an innovation system as defined by Innovaton360

Managing strategic initiatives and innovation projects also calls for key performance indicators (KPIs). The use of KPIs is essential to following, judging, and making decisions about prioritized projects, including starting projects, granting resources, adjusting resources, stopping, pausing, or launching projects, and even speeding up or slowing down projects. Typically, KPIs can be divided based on the innovation system; as illustrated in figure 14, they could be related to insights, exploration, decision, or execution. In portfolio management, KPIs would typically be related to decisions and their execution, whereas execution is related to development and commercialization. For example,

- **Decisions** can be followed by a number of tested ideas in relation to decided ideas.

- **Development** can be actual cost in relation to budget.

- **Commercialization** can be new growth, new gross margin, or new customers in relation to existing growth, margins, and customer acquisition.

It is almost impossible to provide guidelines regarding KPIs, but generally speaking, each horizon uses a different target, and a KPI is not always about reaching and surpassing a specific target—often it can be a range rather than a specific target. As an example, let's consider whether it's good to have many ideas that are turned into projects. You might answer "not necessarily," as that might mean that you did not fail often enough—you didn't learn enough, you didn't test enough new things and so on. However, the opposite would also not make sense, where nothing turns into a project. So there has to be a range to aim for, and that range is dependent on the horizon that you are working in. In the first horizon, an idea requires less testing, while in the third horizon many more tests are required and fewer ideas can turn into projects.

One practical and simplified way of managing innovation projects is to classify them into horizons and time spans, in order to map them to strategic initiatives. In the third horizon, it might just be for learning and fuzzy ideas related to one specific strategic initiative, resulting in more tangible H2 and H1 business projects. figure 15 illustrates the concept of mapping projects to strategic initiatives, different horizons and time spans. Something that has been proven in practice to help leaders and managers understand how to manage and prioritize their projects over time.

108

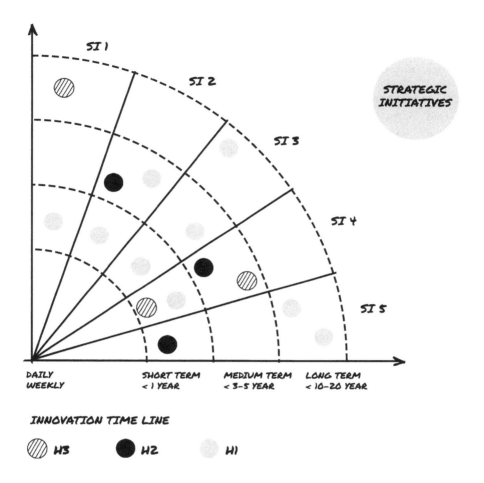

Figure 15. How to manage strategic initiatives and projects.

7.2   Managing Platform Development

Platform management is essential to maintaining development efficiency. Platforms can be both hard and/or soft platforms.

Soft platforms are what we also call change platforms, the prerequisite for change. Soft platforms are discussed in greater detail in chapter 8, "Leading Change for Innovation – UPACS" and Chapter 9, "Organizational Design".

109

Hard platforms can be physical, but also logical (software) platforms, such as source code libraries in the IT industry, Apple Store, GitHub for version management and sharing software components, blueprints in construction and manufacturing, and new initiatives such as blockchain technology.

Platform management, especially hard platform management, is sometimes referred to as Product Information Management and Product Life Cycle Management. Hard platforms typically link to sustainability and design for the "reduce, reuse, and recycle" approach, as well as driving or coordinating everything from de facto standards to ISO standards.

To illustrate how a platform can be used, let's take blockchain technology as an example:

Blockchain driving external transformation – External transformation is mainly driven by how effectively the company customize platforms, products and services improving customer experience by engaging and gathering insights from the customer base. Customers and generally external engagement is a key feature of cryptocurrencies and blockchain technologies application. There are several business models that has been impacted by external engagement-driven blockchain applications, for example Augur (https://augur.net/) which is a decentralized prediction market who engage its customers in providing predictions and forecasts on given events. It is powered by an ethereum based token called augur which is listed on major exchange.

Blockchain driving internal transformation – Internal transformation is about how to organize for knowledge creation and sharing, production, process development and redesign supply, and cross-border learning. Process improvement and business transformation is one of the key application areas of blockchain and cryptocurrencies. At this writing, blockchain is reshaping the back office of many banks and financial institutions. Ripple (https://www.ripple.com/), for example, is a cryptocurrency specialized in cross-border settlements that has already been adopted by 75 banks worldwide, among them UBS, Standard Chartered, Santander, and Westpac.

Blockchain driving market expansion – Market expansion is affected by capabilities connected with value proposition of platforms, products, and services, and by how effectively we use channels, brand, and connect with the external environment. An interesting application of blockchain technologies for market expansion is IOTA (https://iota.org/), an innovative new distributed ledger technology that functions as the backbone of the Internet of Things (IoT). The technology behind IOTA is called the Tangle and is completely new in respect to bitcoin and ethereum. Its application is still under technical scrutiny; nevertheless, its impact on IoT could be very interesting. IOTA can work off the internet and enable autonomous interactions between various IoT devices, completing underlined transactions. For example, networks of IOTA-enabled IoT devices can exchange information about pricing and settle transactions without human intervention and without fees.

Blockchain driving increased profits – Increased profits is mainly driven from how we capture value, learning from our customers and internal assets, repositioning our processes, and leveraging organizations. Something interesting has been done by Numer.ai (https://numer.ai/), a new kind of hedge fund built by a network of data and artificial intelligence scientists, who contribute trading strategies and are paid with "numeraire" tokens.

Today, many companies are actually acting and planning based on both logical and physical platforms with defined components, architecture, interoperability and interchangeability of components.

The intent of building on logical and physical platforms and components is to reduce time and money spent as well as quality problems, in order to focus on what really makes a difference as new innovations are tested and eventually scaled up internationally. Often new innovations can be tested and scaled up based in large part on existing flexible technology, rather than re-inventing the wheel time after time.

CHAPTER 8
LEADING CHANGE FOR INNOVATION

There are three aspects of leading change for innovation that according to our experiences we think are both essential and really useful to succeed; The first is about coping with the inherent challenges of change, where we apply the UPACS model, the second is about managing stakeholders for radical innovation and the third is about team development.

8.1   Manage the challenges through UPACS

To lead change to promote innovation, we have defined a change management model that we call *UPACS*: UPACS stand for: Uncertainty, Paradoxes, Ambiguity, Complexity, and Speed.

This type of leadership is highly demanding, as it calls for the simultaneous deployment of both abilities and high aspirations. As mentioned in earlier chapters, we categorize development into either business projects or change projects. Business projects concern the business itself, including products, services, facilities, marketing, sales, supply, and so on. We organize business projects into portfolios and use portfolio management techniques to manage them. Change projects relate to aspiration and ability, including leadership, culture, organization, roles, incentives, talent management, and so on. We organize change projects into change programs and implement a change management approach to oversee them.

First, let's just restate that an organization is not a monolith. It consists of humans, humans with different perceptions, aspirations, and abilities. Why is it important to restate this? Because in most of the strategy work we have seen in the past, this is an assumption: if you start by understanding the nature of the organization and people, you will also be able to handle their complexity using strengths as strengths and not as disadvantages.

113

One example is a recruitment and staffing company that was stuck in incremental market reading that failed over and over again, even though they had the right strategy—digitalization—in place. Why? Because the organization could not handle it yet, and no one actually considered the organization as consisting of several individual parts. Instead, the project received more overall investment, eventually complemented with just a few external resources (a digitalization specialist) that were all totally assimilated into the company's old way of working within just a few months. The breakdown was total, with no working systems and much internal frustration. As a result, the CEO dismissed a number of senior managers. But by assessing and measuring aspiration and ability in each part of the organization, it was possible to identify the part of the organization that had the aspiration and ability to cope with the UPACS challenges surrounding the strategy. This group could actually succeed and show the way from (in this case) Horizon 2 to Horizon 1, where the same change was implemented throughout the company. The specific challenges they faced within UPACS were:

Uncertainty: Can we digitalize, for instance, the interview process, which is very time consuming? As a second step, can we add extra services to the talent market with a digital AI-based robot providing coaching on interviewing? How do we build a data structure that will last? Is that possible? Is it desirable?

Paradoxes: People want the soft skills of a human interviewing and selecting candidates, but at the same time they want the accuracy and speed of computerized decisions.

Ambiguity: Internal staff and management want to keep their jobs, but at the same time the company needs a new level of efficiency to compete.

Complexity: Linking all candidate data with client data and codified interviews and making computerized decisions that are well documented and accurate is very complex and it is easy loose important details on the way. Maintaining compliance with new regulations regarding data protection and sustainability reporting makes it even more complex, as does the potential use of artificial intelligence and communication bots.

Speed is increasing in every aspect of the industry, from four-to-six-month recruitment cycles to cycles of less than one or two months. Accessibility and visualization is required by both clients and the talent, calling for the need to provide updates in real time.

By the end of the day the company was able to digitalize, using the business unit that had the aspiration and ability that was most suited to the task. But the innovation for the third horizon only succeeded when a centralized innovation task force was established, experimenting and learning about innovations like machine learning (advanced artificial intelligence) and bots for communication.

8.2   Manage your Stakeholders for Radical Innovation

When working with change, stakeholder management is essential to creating everything from insights to alignment and aspiration. It is the best and only approach to managing innovation from the first known horizon to radical innovation in the second and third horizon, where the only thing you can be sure of is uncertainty and the prospect of many failures before breakthroughs are generated. In our experience, leaders and organizations fail to reach regular breakthroughs for these (among other) reasons:

1. They do not believe in breakthroughs and they do not commit themselves to breakthrough goals.

2. They fail to communicate the goals and get other people involved.

3. They continue to do what they have always done before.

4. They do not like resistance, failure, or defeat, and they often interpret them as proof or a reason why they should not continue or persevere.

5. They lack perseverance. They are not able to face zero results for any extended period of time. Compromise seems easier or more reasonable. They fail to recognize the fact that breakthroughs do not occur on a linear basis. Breakthroughs are highly unpredictable.

The challenge lies in our own thinking. Every fiber of our body and mind wants to resist. All systems are self-preserving. At the same time, everything around us is in constant change.

Why is it important to change in order to succeed with radical innovation? The answer is because it is the hardest part. From an aspirational and ability perspective, changing and optimizing the current business is pretty straightforward and can be integrated as part of any business and under any leadership. And, of course, it is important to build ability and drive the aspiration for innovation in the first horizon too. But without the second and third horizons you will most likely sooner or later be out of business, no matter what business you're in, due to the rapid change we are seeing in today's markets. So, a tolerance for and willingness to change is a critical mindset for any business leader.

To prepare an organization for radical innovation, we have identified ten first steps to take:

1. Select the right group, based on aspiration and ability (through assessment, as described in the first volume of this book series). Both the aspiration and the collective ability are cornerstones in succeeding with challenging tasks like radical innovation in the second and third horizon.

2. Identify and establish a strategic initiative—an inspiring possibility and a shared background. Setting up a purpose, enrolling for reaching goals and defining a fulfilling vision to motivate and establish perseverance.

3. Establish radical breakthrough goals. Enroll and communicate. Communication should be within the group but also externally to establish a sense of urgency and true commitment.

4. Get people involved. Get quick wins. Communicate, build confidence, and celebrate, as this will prepare for failures and challenges that need to be overcome.

5. Coach and train around aspiration and abilities for radical innovation

6. (see Table 1).

7. Take action and generate results. It is important to call for action, to do things and feel that you do things. Always set goals, even short-term, easy-to-reach goals, as it makes it easier to believe in the long-term, more ambitious goals.

8. Deal directly with unexpected outcomes. It will happen, deal quickly and accept. Learn from mistakes and encourage failure and unexpected results.

9. Persevere. Never give up.

10. Implement a full innovation system (Volume 3 of this book series) that are linked to one or two strategic initiatives after the first successfully commercialized innovation project.

11. Reassess (Volume 1 of this book series), adjust, and take the change to the next level.

What we have seen in projects is that enrolling, handling the unexpected, and perseverance are the hardest parts. Enrolling is about getting people involved and to achieve that, communicating is of utmost importance. Communication is a primary action that drives all other actions. One's own thought process is a primary action: a conversation with oneself, conscious or unconscious, takes place before any other actions can take place. To enroll means to communicate with others in such a way that they see the same possibilities that you do, so they become ready to make commitments. Some examples of this communication and enrollment process include talking about goals, declaring commitments, and/ or inviting others to consider new possibilities. Establishing common ground, inviting and making your own commitments, and visualizing success are also effective tools for enrollment.

Beware: if you do not like resistance, failure, or problems, you may well find yourself using them as a rationale for not continuing to deal with unexpected outcomes. Breakthroughs occur as a consequence of radical actions that generate a series of successes and failures. Action is required, either to deal with the failures or to utilize the successes. The very first action of setting new goals may create new possibilities and enthusiasm in some people, while causing stress, problems, and anxiety in others. A good leader must maintain enthusiasm, prepare for failure, visualize success, and keep motivating people. Never be afraid of declaring something a breakdown, learning from it, celebrating success, and building legends and stories to use for future inspiration.

Lack of perseverance is another common reason why people do not perform better than they do. Few people, including senior management, can face zero results for any extended period of time. In these situations, compromise seems easier and more reasonable and, in many cases, seems plainly to make sense. Should one always persevere at all cost? No, of course not—often it is reasonable to accept failure and move on. But let's put it this way: Fail often but fail fast! Learn from it and prepare for the next thing, shaping your own future.

8.3   Develop the right team(s)

Besides establishing purpose, aspiration, and abilities such as capabilities and the right mix of personas, most innovation teams will pass through similar stages of development. Simultaneously with developing new level of consciousness, often ranging from "unconscious incompetence" to "conscious competence" (see figure 16), the group passes through the stages of group formation. Experience

117

shows that it is often easy in the beginning, when most members of a group are not aware of what is going to happen and are full of enthusiasm—or at least not counterproductive. However, once the group forms and develops its ability and aspiration, frustration can also develop. It is extremely important to link group members to purpose, and carefully enroll and coach them as well as their leaders to maintain their belief that working systematically and succeeding with breakthroughs is possible.

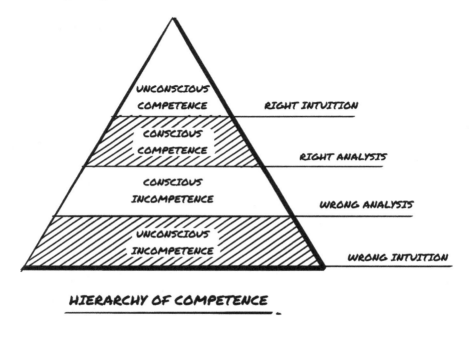

Figure 16: The four stages of competence (Source: Burch, 1978). The Four Stages of competence provides a model for learning. It suggests that individuals are initially unaware of how little they know, or unconscious of their own incompetence. As they recognize their incompetence, they consciously acquire a skill, then consciously use it. Ultimately, the skill can be utilized unconsciously: the individual is then said to have acquired unconscious competence.

As described earlier, groups typically pass through the stages of forming, storming, norming, performing, and potentially adjourning (Tuckman, 1965, 1977). In each of these phases, the development of aspiration and ability will prolong the phase and lengthen the time before the group can perform effectively. At the same time, working groups that are equipped to run innovation are necessary, another reason to not form new groups for each purpose but to instead reach out to established teams in the organization who can be trained until success stories and proofs can be communicated. Forming new groups to work with innovation in the second and third horizon will fail for three reasons:

- It is the first time the organization has tried radical innovation and the group does neither have basic aspirations nor ability, or

- The group has not yet formed its working dynamics and is not skilled and properly trained in radical innovation, or

- The mix of people is not right.

Therefore, we advise finding, or building, a team of radical innovators, training and coaching them, giving them freedom under a manager with the right leadership skills (see Table 1), and then building up success stories and role models step by step. This process will both institutionalize an innovation system (which will be discussed further in chapter 9) as either a centralized unit or one/several satellites and work on constant improvements (Horizon 1) within the regular business by inspiring, training, coaching, and rewarding or otherwise incentivizing improvements and the behavior that supports them.

Another interesting aspect of team development, and a possibility to consider, is how to nurture cross-fertilization or intersectional thinking, not only through diversity of personas but also through background and expert knowledge in different areas. Many breakthroughs are made by people outside traditional fields, where people with insights and perspectives challenge the accepted paradigms that are taken for granted within the field.

CHAPTER 9
ORGANIZATIONAL DESIGN

In many assignments, we see that the client has already established an innovation center, or may be planning to do so. But often such centers do not deliver on expectations and instead can turn out to be very cost inefficient structures that clash with the rest of the organization. However, ignoring innovation and the capability it can give an organization is not a viable option in today's marketplace. So, the question is, how can we better design such capabilities to drive successful innovation?

First let´s recap some of the basic innovation concepts we've discussed so far. The first horizon (H1) concerns smaller, incremental innovations that build on existing business models, extending the existing S-curve of the company. These can normally be accomplished with little structural change or lead time. The second horizon (H2) is more creative and proactive and involves expanding and building new businesses into new directions. The third horizon (H3) is sometimes characterized as "moon shots" or "skunk works." This is a much more explorative approach to future S-curves, which can be commercialized in H2 and end up producing significant cash flows in H1. Ideally, a company should be working on all three horizons simultaneously.

The biggest failure of many contemporary strategies is that they are stuck in H1. Some studies indicate that up to 99 percent of businesses are trapped in H1 due to "spiral staircase" leadership in which, in the interest of safety and risk aversion, leaders mandate step-by-step projects with narrowly-defined goals and a predictable return on investment (ROI). This strategy has also been compared to arranging deckchairs on the Titanic, a futile and trivial action in the face of an impending catastrophe. In this scenario, large H1 projects tend to get prioritized to such an extent that they can generate internal traffic jams, holding back H2 or H3 projects that must vie for the same resources. The result is that the go-ahead is given to projects that are too numerous, too big, and too cautious to create real value for the firm or its customers.

A more successful approach is seen in companies that deploy their limited resources more optimally by simultaneously nurturing today's profit (H1), developing new ideas for tomorrow's profit and market share (H2), and taking part in building the future (H3). To link strategic direction and business modeling in a hypercompetitive market with the change and transformation programs that drive successful business development on several horizons, the successful leader must have a thorough understanding of what innovation management means within the context of his or her own organization.

9.1 Setting Strategic Goals and Making the Correct Design Choices

To gain a full understanding of what organizational design, or establishing an innovation center could mean to an organization, we must first define the strategic goals that might give the desired direction and support the necessary decision making. According to the work of Peet van Biljon, there are at least ten strategic goals that could—on their own or in combination—drive an organization to establish an innovation center:

1. Create a critical mass of skills and knowledge

2. Obtain new consumer/user insights

3. Adopt and adapt new technologies

4. Collaborate externally (external networks, partnerships, JVs)

5. Identify new business opportunities

6. Establish a footprint in new or emerging markets

7. Scale innovations faster

8. Build a test bed for rapid experimentation

9. Provide a showcase of new offerings

10. Create a base for future acquisitions

Outlining your organization's strategic goals is the first step to follow when considering possible choices for designing its innovation strategy. Once the goals are clear, then the design process can move forward.

Based on the work of Peet van Biljon and Magnus Penker, there are a number of design choices to be made:

- How to link to a parent company's/owner's growth strategy
- Choice of geographic location
- Governance and reporting structures
- Details of parent involvement (formal and informal)
- Operating model
- Parent's involvement in major decisions
- Talent management, such as talent identification, selection, and incentives

When designing an organization's innovation strategy, its strengths and weaknesses need be considered, and not just at the organizational level, but also by examining innovation characteristics throughout the organization, including team leadership, strategy for innovation, capabilities, and competences for adopting the best solutions.

Design decisions should also be based on an external and internal analysis as well as on initial plans for removing blockages and amplifying the strategic direction of the organization. As discussed in an earlier chapter, typically these decisions are based on one of three approaches:

1. Best Fit, where decisions are based on how the current situation looks and what's possible without any major changes. Typically, these decisions are based on the current conscious strategy, leadership, type of innovation, and the capabilities and competences that need to be strengthened.

2. Best in Class, where decisions are based on the best companies that have the same strategic intent that you do, regardless of their industry. These recommendations focus on the changes needed in strategy, leadership, type of innovation, personas (the culture), capabilities, and competences that will bring your company in alignment with these "best-in-class" companies.

3. Resource-based View, where decisions are based on the company's current capabilities, personas, and competences, and focus on what is realistically possible and how that can be aligned with the company's existing overall strategic direction.

9.2 Organizational Principles for Innovation Centers

When it comes to implementing an innovation center, there are usually three possible organization designs to choose from, and the decision on which to apply should be made based on all of the work described so far: the organization's strategic goal, the design choice, the analysis of the internal and external context, and the decision to use one of the three approaches outlined above: Best Fit, Best in Class, or Resource-based View. The three possible organizational designs are:

- as a central department
- as a fully integrated unit within the existing organizational chart
- as several collaborating satellites.

An innovation center could also be implemented as a combination of these.

Each model has its pros and cons. The centralized model is efficient, but innovation often occurs in other parts of the business or in the marketplace. An integrated innovation unit is easier to implement in first horizon strategies, but very often hard or impossible to execute efficiently in second and third horizons due to daily priorities. Collaborating satellites are a mix of both and can be very efficient, but it can be hard to coordinate among them, as they tend to be highly autonomous or allied with a specific part of the market or the organization.

Every organization must choose their own specific design among these options based on its own horizon strategy, its industry and market, current level of innovation, and other unique internal and external factors. In all cases, after many years working with companies of all sizes in many different markets, we have found that innovation centers, like innovation systems, are often better implemented in small steps and not as a formal, full-blown initiative from day one.

CHAPTER 10

ARTIFICIAL INTELLIGENCE AND INNOVATION – AN EXECUTIVE'S TECH GUIDE BEYOND RHETORIC

You must not fight too often with one enemy, or you will teach him all your art of war.

— *Napoleon Bonaparte*

As we said in the introduction to this book, AI is already a powerful engine for innovation and will continue to be so in the years ahead. Yet not enough has been written on this vital topic, apart from dire warnings and dystopian or opportunistic prophecies. This is why we present this "Executive's tech guide beyond rhetoric" for you to read, and this is also why we chosen to be rather technical and look under the hood to really figure out how it works and how it will impact. Both limitations and possibilities are explored.

Note: If you are not yet ready for a deep dive into the subject of AI, please just leave this chapter for now, and jump directly to the epilogue and conclusions chapter.

Not long ago one of our clients, a highly skilled former top consultant, now a seasoned industry leader, asked for *Artificial Intelligence for Dummies*. An interesting question for a highly skilled and insightful person to ask, and somewhat reminiscent of the internet hype of the 90s, when firms made fortunes via fundraising and spectacular dud projects for the new economy. Are our high expectations of AI akin to the folly of the crowd in *The Emperor's New Clothes*, the Hans Christian Andersen tale of two weavers who promise an emperor a new suit of clothes which they claim is invisible to those who are unfit for their positions. When the emperor parades before his subjects in his new clothes, no one dares to say that they do not see clothes on him for fear that they will be seen as "unfit for their positions, stupid, or incompetent." But, finally, a child cries out, "But he isn't wearing anything at all!"

My esteemed client asked if there were an *Artificial Intelligence for Dummies* book, because it feels just like in the 90s when there were spectacular stories of new technology, and a threatening sense of not understanding it—and we might very well end up in the same predicament that we did then. The technology matured, but many of the promises that were made were broken. Still, a few new enterprises, on a very large scale, grew as a result of the investments and technology that emerged during the 90s, and this scenario has repeated throughout history. Technology, investment, and brave leadership have all reshaped the future in times when promises and dreams were broken. At the same time, coincidences have often played a role in history and outcomes. This is also why we have devoted a whole, and fairly deep, chapter on Artificial Intelligence.

One example of how technology and coincidence most likely changed history is the story of the Enigma. The Enigma machine was a piece of encryption hardware invented by a German and finally penetrated by Britain's code breakers to decipher German signals traffic during World War Two. It has been claimed that as a result of the information gained by deciphering this device, hostilities between Germany and the Allied forces were curtailed by two years. What would have happened if the British code breakers had not cracked it? We do not know, but what we do know is that it was cracked by a number of skilled mathematicians, including Alan Turing, and that their breakthrough was reached by, among other things, acquiring this stolen Enigma and using a new technology called the "Bombe" (BBC, 2017).

While technology, strategy, and knowledge can change the course of history, sometimes in combination with random events, adversaries also learn from each other, whereby advantages are narrowed and balance is eventually restored until the next tipping point is reached due to temporarily advantages. Or, as Napoleon Bonaparte put it, "You must not fight too often with one enemy, or you will teach him all your art of war."

Innovation is about gaining, sustaining, and using advantages for as long as possible while, at the same time, gaining knowledge for future eventualities without exactly knowing if, when, or how it will be used.

Now to artificial intelligence: Ask yourself in which horizon AI resides, and how you should approach and, if possible, use it. To guide you when answering this question, we will walk through five steps in order to investigate, understand, and project the possibilities of using artificial intelligence in business. These will be based on a combination of technology insights and practical experience and will be expressed in non-technical language, with pros and cons. Most importantly, it will omit dystopian scenarios. When reading the five steps, keep in mind that the growth of patent applications and investments in artificial intelligence in United States and China is tremendous—with 28,000 filed patents, 35,000 AI companies, and over $20B USD in investments from 2016 alone, which is projected to boost global GDP by $16T (*The Economist*, 2017). The most likely reason behind the growing interest in AI is the growing computing power and new computer architecture, which can perform vector operations much better (important for AI) than traditional computer architecture. It is not overly bold to state that we will see totally new computer architecture and algorithms taking AI even further than today and that you will benefit from getting ready for this future.

10.1 What Is Artificial Intelligence and Machine Learning, and How Does It Work?

Over the decades, there have been a number of artificial intelligence approaches, from rule-based systems, to conclusions being drawn from a set of predefined rules, to self-learning systems (so-called machine learning). With today's computer power and new computer architectures handling vector calculations more efficiently than ever before, self-learning systems have become of great interest. At the moment, the most well-recognized method for learning is the artificial neuron network (ANN), which is based on the basic principles of how the brain works.

10.1.1.1 The Brain

The core component of the nervous system in general, and the brain in particular, is the neuron (or nerve cell). A neuron is an electrically excitable cell that processes and transmits information by electro-chemical signaling. The average human brain has about 100 billion neurons and each neuron can be connected to up to 10,000 other neurons, passing signals to each other via as many as 1,000 trillion synaptic connections (see figure 17 for an illustration). An ANN is built up by neurons and the weighted connections between them (the equivalent to synapses) and reacts to inputs by giving an output.

129

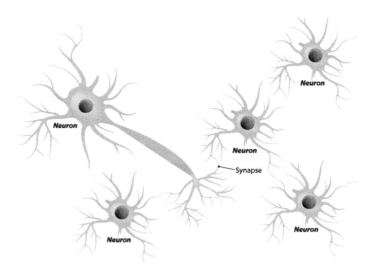

Figure 17: A sketch of neurons and how they are connected by synapses in the brain

10.1.1.2 The Black Box

An Artificial Neuron Network (ANN) is basically a "black box" with a set of inputs (a vector or an array of inputs) and a set of outputs (a vector, or an array of outputs), as shown in figure 18. The set of inputs consists of a number of values, normally between 0 and 1 (e.g., 0.3; 0.4; 0.7; 0.1) and a number of outputs, normally also between 0 and 1. The ANN is not intelligent from the beginning: it needs to learn from data (a process called propagation) to act in what is perceived as an intelligent way of making, for example, decisions and forecasts. You could say that, in its simplest form, an ANN is a function of an input vector delivering an output vector.

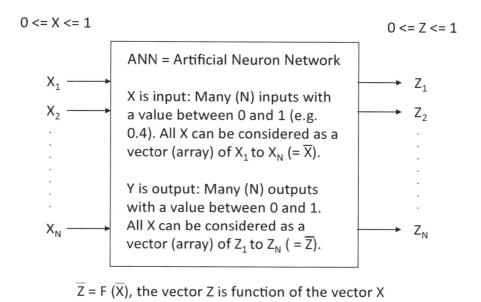

$\overline{Z} = F\ (\overline{X})$, the vector Z is function of the vector X

Figure18: The basic principles of an Artificial Neuron Network (ANN)

In ANNs, there are a number of input neurons and a number of outputs—it does not have to be the same number. For example, one application determines when to run marketing campaigns to drive online sales. When sending marketing messages out, you will gather data on conversion rates (actual sales in relation to the size of the audience) and the time when the campaign was sent. If you have a lot of data on conversion rates and dates (including both the day and time), you can use an ANN to predict the best day and time of day to send a campaign to get the best conversion rate. The input is time (day of the week and time of day) and the conversion rate. The output is the time at which to send a new campaign in order to gain the maximum conversion rate. To make this possible, you need to convert the input variable to a number (X), with a value between 0 and 1, so that you get a number for the output variable (Z), with a value between 0 and 1, that can translate to days and time of the day. Now, it might not be especially easy or even possible to predict the conversion rate based only on the time that a campaign is sent. So, you can add more inputs, such as:

- Length of the campaign (word count)

131

- Click rate

- Weather conditions

- Length of the headline

- Colors used

- Price range

- The price in relation to competitors (via price comparison sites)

- If the products are in stock

- Delivery terms and conditions

- Special deals and discounts

Defining the input format, defining output format, and mining past data (input and output) is the key to machine learning. Besides the input, output, and the learned data, the ANN also needs to be designed to optimally solve the task.

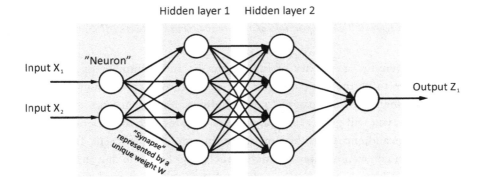

Figure 19: Many layers of neurons, forming a deep learning system

10.1.1.3   Design: Hidden Layers

As figure 19 shows, there are several layers of neurons, connected via "synapses," between the input layer of neurons and the output layer of neurons. When there are many layers, more complicated tasks can potentially be undertaken, and it is called deep learning. There is no rule about the number of layers or the number of neurons in each layer: this is a design question and is determined via many tests on past data.

In figure 20, you can see how the neurons are connected. Every neuron is connected to all other neurons in the layer before, and every connection has a weight (0 is used for a "non-connection"). The job of the neuron is to summarize all inputs by first weighting every input and then summarizing it. The sum of all weighted inputs is then transformed into a number between 0 and 1 (sometimes -1 to 1) that is sent forward to the next layer, and to the next layer, until it arrives in the last output layer, where the output is normally between 0 and 1. The function used for transforming an input to an output in each neuron is called an activation function.

10.1.1.4   Design: The Activation Function

Until recently, sigmoid or hyperbolic tangents were used exclusively, but a Rectified Linear Unit (ReLU) is now also a common activation function in the hidden layers. According to data scientists C. Zhang and P. C. Woodland (2015), it is also possible to parameterize the activation functions and thereby gain a better result for various applications, such as speech recognition. Both have their pros and cons, which will be not discussed here. However, it is reasonable to draw the conclusion that the activation function will be developed further, for different applications and hardware architectures, and hardware will be created to carry out the calculations, as these are time-consuming calculations when the ANN is "learning."

10.1.1.5   Design: Backward Propagation of
Errors and Gradient Descent

Backpropagation, or backward propagation of errors, is a method where the result in the output layer (Z with a ^, as shown in figure 20) is compared with the expected result from the learning data (Z) and the difference is used to adjust the weights in the neural network. The algorithm used to adjust the weights is called gradient descent, and there are several approaches to doing this. As with the activation function, the selection of the algorithm depends on the application. Sometimes stochastic methods are used to experiment with different weights. As with the case of activation functions, backward propagation of errors and gradient descent are subject to development and also depend on the application for which the ANN is being developed.

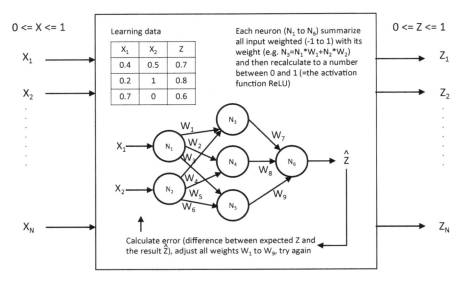

Figure 20: An ANN with several layers, weights, and learning data. Backpropagation adjusts the weights based on error calculations.

10.1.1.6 Design: Recurrent Neural Network

One issue with the ANN is that, in its basic construction, it does not work optimally for consecutive sequences, such as text, speech, video, and audio. Therefore, the recurrent neural network (RNN) was developed using both predictions (the result) and earlier data as inputs. Typically, you develop several ANNs with functions for Forget, Select, and Ignore based on earlier data. This is very useful for anything embedded in time, such as text, speech, video, and audio recognition, as well as production and social interaction. It is most likely that we will see lots of ANNs organized into larger nets to solve more complex tasks in the future.

10.2 What Artificial Intelligence and Deep Learning Can Do for You

When an ANN is trained, the actual use of the net is very efficient and does not require a lot of hardware. ANNs can be deployed on hardware, such as watches, sensors, and other small circuits, with a CPU and internet connection. This can lead to disruptions in many industries and business models, such as heating or cooling systems for homes and industries, smart homes, and logistics and transportation of goods. Imagine reducing the amount of electricity needed to run your heating system at home or the cooling system for a computer farm by 40 to 70 percent just by adding AI. The same goes for many other applications.

By using inexpensive, standardized hardware to run the ANNs, and using internet connections for the hardware's intensive deep learning, the price of these ANN-assisted devices can be reduced to next to nothing and, at the same time, you can get even more learning data from several local installations. This makes it possible to compile better learnings and provide them back to local, simple pieces of hardware though internet connections. The growth of the Internet of Things (IoT) and Industrial Internet of Things (IIoT), combined with centralized data collection, deep learning, and localized software propagation, is most likely a trend that will lead to the disruption of many business models with new revenue streams via subscriptions, significantly more efficient operations and maintenance, smarter functions, higher security, and the greater potential to be a part of large networks that optimize resources in new ways by sharing economic models. At the same time, they also raise new concerns about integrity and cybersecurity, and all forces have counterforces. It is most likely that we will see closed systems, or trusted communities, to a greater extent than before.

10.2.1.1 More Applications

Examples of other applications in which ANNs have proven to be useful are diagnosing cancer, telemedicine, translating texts written in natural languages, recognizing objects in enormous masses of visual data and other advanced search tasks, providing automated advice in online help desks, pricing, trading, and, recently, self-driving cars, all of which seem promising for the future. Common to all these applications is the need to be able to define important inputs that drive a result (reasonably closed loop systems) and the need for access to a lot of past data of inputs and outputs (or expected outputs). This need for inputs and expected outputs for learning in an ANN network has garnered great interest, such as in the example of home heating or cooling systems, where millions of users can cooperate via the internet to gather data and gain efficiencies superior to alternative approaches. Another emerging trend is reinforcement learning with rewards, which is inspired by behavioral psychology and concerned with how software agents ought to take actions in a given environment so as to maximize some notion of cumulative reward. Reinforcement learning is conducted without any correct input/output pairs and is used in experiments with self-driving cars.

Both data collected through the internet and reinforcement learning could be viewed as machine innovation, most likely in the first horizon. Now, you might ask, why not in the second and third horizon? There are at least two issues that make machine innovation in Horizon 2 and 3 pretty difficult:

- Diversified input data, which is essential, is hard to secure.

- Complex learning requires stochastic models that are based on the random and random is, at the moment, not possible to simulate for computers (we are close to achieving it, but even the enormous amount of random data needed in complex deep learning might not be enough).

Let's come back to the above discussion later. For now, the point is that diversified data, large amounts of data, and random data are important keys to driving deep learning toward self-innovation and are not just improvements in the first horizon.

10.2.1.2 Intersectional Thinking

ANNs combined with IoT, IIoT, robotics, nanotechnology, biotech, and medtech seem promising. Earlier patterns suggest that innovations are often created in the intersection of disciplines—often by outsiders who do not expect to create them, such as when they are trying to improve something rather than make something new and unconventional. A good example is the discovery of penicillin. According to the Society for Interdisciplinary Studies (2017), the photocopier was invented by a lawyer, color film by a concert violinist, and the oil refinery by a racing driver. So it is not brave to guess that some new groundbreaking inventions will be made by outsiders and in the intersection of all-new disciplines.

10.2.1.3 Level of Applications

According to Anand Rao (2017), artificial intelligence business applications can be divided into three categories:

- Assisted intelligence, now widely available, improves what people and organizations are already doing.

- Augmented intelligence, emerging today, enables organizations and people to do things they couldn't otherwise do.

• Autonomous intelligence, being developed for the future, creates and deploys machines that act on their own.

These categories are useful because they help us to scope who will use the technology in relation to humans and businesses. Typically, assisted intelligence is used for decision-making, removing unnecessary administrative tasks, and making tasks faster, which creates space and opportunity for social engagement, experience, and human judgment. Augmented intelligence is an extension and, indeed, very interesting, as it is already in use by many of our clients with good results. This is typically used for remote proactive maintenance of factories, production cells, and other complex systems, such as lift systems, and reduces the cost of maintenance substantially. Another typical area for augmentation is the service industry, where consultants, lawyers, doctors, auditors, and other knowledge workers can give faster, more accurate, and more precise advice when using AI to extend their ability. Autonomous intelligence is already here with simpler applications, such as robotic lawn mowers, and we can expect to see many more applications of greater complexity in the coming years.

10.2.1.4   Innovation and AI

Some of the real breakthroughs in AI were when AI won world championships in chess and GO. Deep learning is best applied when there is clear input, clear output, and a lot of accessible data with variations. When we know what we want (defined output), AI works very well and drives innovation in the first horizon. This also leads to new business models in the second horizon with totally new applications, as in the example of reducing costs and introducing subscription models based on data from a community.

But can AI be used to drive innovation without human intervention? The problem with AI is that it needs to be fed with defined inputs and expected outputs, as well as a lot of diversified data. There are currently attempts to use AI to train AI, while other attempts entail using the internet to "scrape" data in enormous amounts, classify it, and then use it. However, it seems that we keep ending the conformity due to AI's difficulty working with unexpected inputs, outputs, and data. In the final chapter of this volume, we will discuss this in a bit more depth. For now, we claim that AI needs humans in order to innovate. And, based on our experience from client assignments, humans need AI to innovate at a certain speed.

As an example of how AI can help human innovation in the second horizon, and eventually the third, let's take our own firm, Innovation360, and the innovation analytic tool, InnoSurvey, as an example. Many years ago, we decided to investigate the linkages between growth and innovation, and ended up with a rather large literature review encompassing the most important innovation management literature of the past 100 years. This work resulted in the Innovation360 Framework, and we immediately started to collect data based on its structure. After a while, Innovation360 Group developed an expert-based analyzer that could generate a 40-page analysis based on data from one company. The collection was made by sending out 92 questions. Based on the framework, we asked managers, employees, and externals about their perception of using digital surveys sent out by e-mail to make it possible to collect large amounts of data for each investigated company, for any and all kinds of organizations. At one point, we decided to launch a free version, based on just one respondent's answer, and, from this, we gathered data from many thousands of companies in 62 countries all over the world. At the beginning, we were afraid of bad quality data from unknown sources (the free version) but after carefully investigating it, using p-value calculus to test data from known sources (from consultancy assignments), we concluded that the quality of unknown sources was good enough.

After a while, we released what we developed—an innovation analytic tool, not just enhancing our ability to make faster and more accurate analysis, but also saving a lot of time for us and our clients. The tool was named InnoSurvey and we started to accredit top consultants all over the world to use it. After just one year, we had 100 licensed practitioners using our solutions in 20 countries and today it is used all over the world. It could have stopped there, but it did not, because we saw new patterns in leadership, strategy, culture, capabilities, and competences to successfully run innovation portfolios over time. We realized that deep learning might give us new insights that the science of the past has not been able to do. After gaining these insights, we started to develop our own gated RNN with supervised learning, controlled by accredited hand-picked internal and external consultants. This project is now scaling up. The hypothesis is that by using the best brains to interpret deep learning results from a large amount of innovation management data, we can innovate the way we consult to clients, not just by automation but also through a totally new kind of analysis: business pattern recognition and advice synthesized by thousands of brains skilled in the art of innovation management.

This case, illustrated by the birth of InnoSurvey and the journey it has taken, shows the potential of combining AI and human power to enable new ways of thinking and working. The next step of this project might very well disrupt the consultancy industry, forming it into orchestrated networks of organizations helping each other out, supported by experienced and highly skilled facilitators instead of classic consultants running projects per hour and charging several clients for the same advice.

10.3   How Artificial Intelligence Can Be Used to Reinvent Your Business Model

The business model is normally considered to consist of an internal part and an external part, where the internal part is the cost structure and the external part is revenue. As an example of how a business model can be reinvented, heating and cooling systems can be equipped with AI technology in a way that substantially reduces the cost of running these systems and raises the possibility of selling subscriptions, where you pay a subscription fee with your own data to get the maximum effect of the system. This is an example of innovation for both cost and revenue. The same goes for the example of InnoSurvey, where less of the users' time is being used and new insights that can change how consultants operate and potentially change their assignments are gained.

One way to look upon business model innovation is through the lens of the Wheel of Innovation, with its 16 aspects and eight groups of aspects, which in Volumes 1 and 2 of this series are referred to as the "eight shadows of innovation." Each of the eight possibilities can be the hunting ground for re-innovating your business model and provides a lens to look through while you are doing that. So, let's walk through each of the eight perspectives and look at some examples of how AI can drive business model innovation.

Market Innovation by AI (a general lens): One tangible and common example of open innovation is when AI is used to facilitate and orchestrate innovation ecosystems with customers, partners, suppliers, and the market in general. Amazon is one of the companies doing this; they use AI to co-create everything from cloud computing services to published books with their audience. Another example is Airbnb and Uber, where the model connects people with resources they want to use—it orchestrates a whole process with AI models to create the best user experience.

Profit Innovation by AI (a general lens): E-commerce providers and retailers are one group that often uses AI for price optimizing, producing stock level forecasts, and purchasing products (especially when there are size, color, model, and session variations). This innovation is directly linked to profit through gross margins and by higher inventory turnover rates.

Internal Transformation by AI (a general lens): Learning organizations constantly challenge themselves by using AI to gain new insights and knowledge. One example is consultancy firms and research centers that use big data and AI to gain new insights that can be used to reach out to the market, keep and grow the market. Another activity where AI is typically used for internal transformation is outsourcing of parts of the value chain, and building and orchestrating the upstream part of the ecosystem. By using AI, these businesses can optimize manufacturing in large ecosystems.

External Transformation by AI (a general lens): This typically engages customers by using and developing offers in a way that creates a superior experience through the whole life cycle, as well as in product and service development. In the gaming industry, "modding" (where users/customers modify games) is a way of engaging hardcore customers in product development. However, in the past, modding has been hard, as it is difficult for customers to code without any guidance. Today, the gaming industry has developed tools for modding and a lot of experiments using deep learning and AI are undertaken. This simplifies the process for modders and also allows mods to modify existing games and develop new games using AI and deep learning.

Offer Innovation (a specific external lens for market growth): Typically, AI is used here to gain data from user behavior in order to offer complementary or new services and products based on earlier behavior. This especially drives growth. Examples of companies using AI in this way are Spotify and Apple Music. Another example is Netflix, which uses data on how we watch movies to actually adapt manuscripts and movie effects, using AI to gain more market share.

Sales Innovation (a specific external lens for profit): This type of innovation is typically used to interact with a large number of customers. AI has revolutionized customer services in many organizations that now use "bots" (automated online customer clerks) for customer care. Bots for customer care and customer service have been proven to be reliable, efficient, fast, and accessible 24/7.

Organizational Innovation (a specific internal lens for profit): This type of augmentation of a human's capacity to provide services is a good example of an AI application. It is used in areas such as consulting, construction, reparation, and translation.

Marketing Innovation (a specific internal lens for market growth): AI is typically used in marketing to innovate how channels and brands are used, an internal process that incorporates the message and position we want in the market. AI has been around for some time in this area with widely used solutions, such as Google Analytics (for understanding digital footprints), Google Trends (for market insights), and a number of specific solutions for analyzing brand awareness and a brand's position.

10.4   Limitations and Business Risk of Using AI and Machine Leaning in Business Development

As described above, input data needs to be formatted as a number between 0 and 1, which is not ideal for some data, for instance, country codes, product IDs, and other data that is not numeric. It is easily adjusted by adding more input nodes but requires more computing power in the learning phase of the ANN.

Another potential weakness is how to treat the out-data when you are not working with probability, as the output is in the range 0 and 1. This can be handled by working with a threshold value (such as 0.5), and letting each neuron have a bias, a constant term that is added to the sum before it goes through the activation function. This also requires more learning, which in turn requires more computer power.

Moreover, many applications require causality (time dependency), such as human interaction, manufacturing, maintenance, and natural languages. A "vanilla" ANN solution will not do, and several neural networks (as mentioned earlier, an RNN) need to be implemented, which in turn calls for more computer power.

There are no rules for the number of neurons in the hidden layers that must be tested: most likely, this is dependent on the application. Again, adding more neurons may increase the capabilities of the model, but requires more computer power.

It is obvious that computer power is the key to an ANN's success. This is something that, together with new architectures and new algorithms, is on its way to being solved—after that, it will no longer be an obstacle.

From a business perspective, in-data is more of a relevant issue. It is not enough to just have a lot of data, popularly called big data: it must be the right data. If we do not have diversified data, the ANN will conform and end up giving conformed outputs, which will not work very well. This issue is of real concern, and data quality must be assessed and complemented with real data, and not just with approximations. Here, stochastic methods and random numbers might play a role, but it is premature to speculate at this stage.

Moreover, machine learning in the business world is also highly dependent on the parameters being used as input data, and sometimes it is not possible to judge this as you simply do not know. Let's say, for instance, that you want support with writing a shareholder purchase agreement (SPA). The process of the merger or acquisition will have an impact on the wording of the paragraphs, based on psychology and not only facts. Writing an SPA is a pretty simple and straightforward process of learning from best practice, but psychology is trickier. Maybe in the future it will be possible to make this type of judgment, but for now it does not really seem to be there. However, there are methods of supervised learning where you can, step-by-step, complement new inputs—these are provided by experts. If you have enough experts, it might very well work (this is also how Google Translate and InnoSurvey are built, with the collaboration of experts in innovation management around the world). Human supervision is one possible way to extend the learning process.

Another issue, which is actually a risk, with AI and business application is de-learning and sabotage. It is possible to feed AI data that will intentionally sabotage the learning process and eventually change behavior, and this can become a huge risk. ANN and more critical applications need to have an "emergency button" to stop the process and must be supervised, not just because of futuristic dystopian scenarios with self-learning war machines, but simply because the learning can be sabotaged—the whole ANN is a black box that cannot be proven or fully validated.

10.5   When Will "The Terminator" Be a Reality?

There are a lot of dystopian prophecies out there. Without either supporting or rejecting them, some background thinking will be provided in this chapter to allow you to make your own judgment.

Computer power, architecture, and algorithms are the most likely candidates to make any kind of judgment that is needed for any kind of rational task. But, several issues have not been solved yet, mostly having to do with not always knowing what input data is needed and, even when we do, not having access to that kind of input data. Now, it has been said that social media and the internet provide us with all we need to know about humanity and behavior and it is just a matter of computer power. However, not all information is accessible via the internet—for a start, consider classified information or business secrets. Even if these are leaked from time to time, new information and knowledge is always being created.

It can be argued that AI can create such new information. Now we come to the core problem for AI, if it is to truly challenge humanity. Why is it that creativity and innovation, regardless of whether it has to do with trade secrets, design, art, national secrets, or disruptive technology, is so hard for AI to simulate? Or, is it? Let's say that it is not hard and it most likely already exists. Perhaps it is in the laboratory, but it is not commercially functional or publicly known in the market at this moment. If or when this happens, then the question is how we will react. A guess is that some humans will find a new way to satisfy our needs and eventually AI will be able to simulate that as well. One thing that seems to differentiate us, as humans, from ANN is random number generation. Random numbers cannot be generated by any known machine in the world's history, and many have tried. There are chip sets on the market with enormous quantities of so-called randomized numbers, but even if they are random, with the random numbers needed by all AI to simulate human creativity they still might not be enough. And, most importantly, they will most likely lead to all AI using the same algorithms and trying to build new algorithms in the same way. However, they are likely to conform or heavily diverge, with the result that humans will still win when it comes to creativity.

143

Besides creativity, it seems, according to Navindra Persaud (2005) in the Department of Neurology at University of Cambridge, that humans use their random-generating neural machinery to make difficult decisions. On the other hand, Persaud (2005) posits that it is also possible that certain people, perhaps those with neurological or psychiatric impairments, are less able or unable to generate random numbers. So, it seems like an ANN cannot replicate all humans, but can potentially replicate some. Moreover, Persaud says that if the random-generating neural machinery is employed in decision-making, its impairment would have profound implications in matters of agency and free will.

My conclusion is that the key to building a "terminator" is to generate true random numbers and I do not believe that will happen. However, I do believe that AI can serve humanity and that we need to proactively create regulations and ethical rules on how to apply it for the best use for humanity in order to avoid catastrophic scenarios due to sabotage or other issues related to a lack of human supervision.

CHAPTER 11
EPILOGUE AND CONCLUSIONS

As we have said before, the Gordian Knot is to use insights you do not yet have in order to utilize strength you do not yet know you have to do something you do not yet know exists. It is no accident that we have arrived at the conclusion of this fifth volume at the intersection of AI and other disruptive technologies, business ethics, and sustainability—here lies an ocean of possibilities and potential traps.

When historians of the future write their assessments of our current era, these topics are very likely to be the defining concern of our time. There is no doubt that the methods we choose for the optimal, ethical, intelligent deployment of AI and other radical technology like Pico Technology, the use of Dark Energy, and our most intractable problems will circumscribe all attempts at innovation for the foreseeable future.

» *AI in the Fourth Industrial Revolution*

Our generation's ongoing revolution is all about consolidating the gains of all past logarithmic advances in technology that redefined mechanical power and energy. The Gordian Knot described above is the true challenge for the leaders of today and tomorrow.

The coalescence of these trends has brought us to the brink of subcutaneous human-AI interface, massively parallel hive minds, DNA-based data storage, and functionally infinite power generators. All the talk about external threats from robots or AI misses the point. As humans and AI work in closer coordination, they have become us and we are them. What machines do in the years ahead, in the form of robotics, AI, IoT, nano devices, and so on, will be fully our responsibility—for good or for evil.

In truth, AI is a bit of a misnomer. There never was and never will be anything

147

artificial about intelligence. It emerges naturally from human consciousness, in all its many varied configurations, from the abacus to IBM's Watson. From the moment humanity carved the first symbols into clay, human intelligence has expanded to fill and subsume the things we have built with our hands.

» *The Urge to Innovate*

The irrepressible urge to innovate has strengthened with the expansion of these complex tools for intellectual inquiry into how the world works. The more we have grown in understanding, the more we want to reshape and develop the world around us.

The heart of the word innovation comes from "nova," Latin for "new." This observation is a helpful reminder that there is nothing inherently good or useful in newness. The value of the new things that we create must be built into innovations during the development process. A better mousetrap is not more valuable just because it is better. It must also fundamentally change human behavior and thought processes, or it will be simply ignored by the overstimulated consumer.

AI and machine learning are critical now because they speak the language of data with greater fluency than human brains do. The more data we have, the better we will be able to understand the true potential of our innovation. We need assistance from those who are native speakers of data, whether they are humans or the creations of human intelligences.

» *The Most Intractable Problems*

The most intractable of those puzzles have foiled humanity's greatest thinkers for thousands of years. How do we prevent man-made disasters? Can we learn from natural ones how to build a more resilient infrastructure? What is the most intelligent, most ethical way to manage the resources of our planet, and soon our solar system, for the greater good? Why do some populations suffer so greatly and is there anything the rest of us can do about that? In essence, it all comes down to: How do we activate the better angels of our nature and come to terms with our conflicting motivations?

The questions of how to preserve a greater portion of revenues as profits and how to scale up operations for stronger potency in the market are still extremely

148

important at the level of an individual organization, in that they represent advances in solving the world's more confounding puzzles. Like water wearing away stone, successful individual innovations can eventually obviate what initially seemed insurmountable.

» *Innovation as a Survival Strategy*

Given the new normal of hyper-competition and economic uncertainty across the globe, firms have a better chance of survival using the hypothesis approach. It creates a framework where you can make serious mistakes with smaller economic impact.

Both Frans Johansson, author of The Medici Effect, and Gary Hamel, author of What Matters Now, agree that one of the most important distinctions between organizations that are more or less innovative is simply the sheer number of ideas that are generated and tested.

By making mistakes as early and cheaply as possible, your research team can afford to test more ideas, hence becoming more innovative.

Regardless of how you proceed in your quest for stronger innovation, growth, and sustainability, it pays to institute a hypothesis-based approach in validated learning cycles.

You can start today on any level: from a single project (i.e., what are the underlying assumptions that produced the hypothesis that this project is our best way forward?) to the macro-level of your company itself (i.e., you can lay out a long-term business model canvas mapping out all of the assumptions built into your business model).

» *Into the Future*

The Innovation360 Group is on the forefront of a seismic disruption of the consulting industry, deploying an analytical approach to producing a culture of innovation, not just individual examples of innovation.

We have implemented a range of tools based on our AI-fueled research to help our clients amplify disruption within their own industries. We provide a deep well of practical knowledge through a support network of top consultants on every continent. Starting from a holistic innovation assessment, organizations discover where they must go next to unlock the potential of their innovation capabilities.

Providing a spark for innovation is not enough. Businesses that lead their verticals in the turbulent global markets have established reliable, reproducible factories for innovation along the three innovation horizons.

It's not luck. Practical, successful innovation is a science, based on data, evidence, and the testing of hypotheticals. That's what Innovation360 does, by means of innovation research, assessments, and measurements.

Information alone can only take you so far, though. What the new world demands is a strategy for managing innovation portfolios that are sustainable, scalable, fast, accurate, and validated. Occupations that derived their value from informational pools, like consultancy, legal services, and medical diagnostic services, are rapidly falling to automation. The future belongs to those who use the most advanced tools to innovate their way into new economics models.

Our working hypothesis is that we have found a more productive way to study the intention, behavior, and results linked to a winning multivariate innovation strategy.

As we continue to strive to uncover and understand innovation more thoroughly, we freely share what we discover with the people who can make innovation happen in the real world.

We empower people to think differently, improve profits, stabilize the global economy, and even figure out how to make our world a better place to live. These are increasingly critical skills in navigating the murky waters of innovation and sustaining business operations into the future.

No one can afford to base these life-and-death decisions on old, outdated assumptions and unrefined data. The ethical, intelligent application of AI, alongside the collective knowledge of human minds, lays out a clear pathway to codify and solve the world's biggest problems.

Have no doubt, our future depends on it.

REFERENCE LIST

Assink, M. 2006. Inhibitors of Disruptive Innovation Capability: A Conceptual Model. *European Journal of Innovation Management* 9 (2): 215–253.

BBC. 2017. Who was Alan Turing? BBC, accessed July 17, 2017. http://www.bbc.co.uk/timelines/z8bgr82.

Baghai, M., Coley, S., & White, D. 1999. *The Alchemy of Growth: Practical Insights for Building the Enduring Enterprise. London*: The Orion Publishing Group Ltd.

Barney J. B., Wright, M., & Ketchen Jr., D.J. 2001. The Resource-Based View of the Firm: Ten Years after 1991. *Journal of Management* 27 (6): 625–641.

Benton, H. H., ed. 1974. *Encyclopaedia Britannica*. 15th ed. London: Encyclopedia Britannica, Inc.

Browne, J., Nuttal, R., & Stadlen, T. (2016). Connect: How Companies Are Succeeding by Engaging Radically with Society. *Public Affairs*.

Burch, N. 1978. Porter, or Ambivalence. *Screen 19* (4): 91–105.

Chamorro-Premuzic, Tomas. 2017. Does Diversity Actually Increase Creativity? JUNE 28. *Harvard Business Review*: Reprint H03R50

Drucker, P. F. 1998. The Discipline of Innovation. *Harvard Business Review* 76 (6): 149–157.

Executive Office of the President. 2016. Artificial Intelligence, Preparing for the Future of Artificial Intelligence Automation, and the Economy. Accessed Aug. 1, 2017. https://obamawhitehouse.archives.gov/blog/2016/12/20/artificial-intelligence-automation-and-economy

Hamel, G. 2012. *What Matters Now: How to Win in a World of Relentless Change, Ferocious Competition, and Unstoppable Innovation.* San Francisco: Jossey-Bass.

Hill, L., Brandeau, G., & Truelove, E. 2014. *Collective Genius: The Art and Practice of Leading Innovation.* United States: Harvard Business Review Press

A. Stachowicz-Stanusch, & W. Amann (Eds.), *Management Education for Corporate Social Performance* (pp. 227-253). Charlotte, NC: Information Age Publishing.

Johansson, F. (2006). *The Medici Effect: What Elephants and Epidemics Can Teach Us about Innovation.* Boston: Harvard Business School Press

Jaruzelski, B., & K. Dehoff. 2010. *The Global Innovation 1000: How the Top Innovators Keep Winning.* New York: Booz & Company, Inc.

Jaruzelski, B., Staack, V., & Goehle, B. Winter 2014. Proven Paths to Innovation Success. *Strategy+Business* 77.

Kelly, T., & Littman, J. 2005. *The Ten Faces of Innovation.* New York: Doubleday.

Kotler, P. T., & Armstrong, G. 2012. *Principles of Marketing, 14th Ed.*, Essex: Person.

Loewe, P., Williamson, P., & Wood, R. C.. 2001. Five Styles of Strategy Innovation and How to Use Them. *European Management Journal* 19 (2): 115–125.

McKinsey & Company. 2009. Enduring Ideas: The Three Horizons of Growth. Accessed June 1, 2017. http://www.mckinsey.com/business-functions/strategy-and-corporate-finance/our-insights/enduring-ideas-the-three-horizons-of-growth.

Ohr, R. C., & K. McFarthing. 2013. Managing Innovation Portfolios: Strategic Portfolio Management, accessed June 1, 2017. http://www.innovationmanagement.se/2013/09/16/managing-innovation-portfolios-strategic-portfolio-management/.

O'Reilly, C., & Tushman, M. 2004. The Ambidextrous Organization. *Harvard Business Review* 82 (4): 74–81.

Penker, M. 2011c. Innovation Key Success Factors for SMEs Acting on Niche Markets. LinkedIn Slideshare, accessed June 29, 2017. https://www.slideshare.

net/magnuspenker/innovation-key-success-factors-for-sme-acting-on-nisch-markets.

Penker, M. 2016. Organizing for Simultaneous Innovation Capability—Key Findings from +1,000 Companies. Presented at the Drucker Forum, Vienna, Nov. 2016.

Penker, M., Jacobson , S., & Junermark , P. (2017). *How to Assess and Measure Business Innovation*. North Charleston, SC: CreateSpace.

Persaud, N. 2005. Humans Can Consciously Generate Random Number Sequences: A Possible Test for Artificial Intelligence. Department of Neurology, University of Cambridge, United Kingdom: *Medical Hypotheses*, Volume 65, Issue 2, Pages 211–214.

Institute for strategy & competitiveness. 2017. The Five Forces. Accessed Dec. 30, 2017. https://www.isc.hbs.edu/strategy/business-strategy/Pages/the-five-forces.aspx

Osterwalder, A., & Y. Pigneur. 2010. Business Model Generation: *A Handbook for Visionaries, Game Changers, and Challengers*. New York: John Wiley and Sons.

Rao, A. 2017. A Strategist's Guide to Artificial Intelligence. *Strategy+Business* 87.

Ries, E. 2011. *The Lean Startup: How Today's Entrepreneurs Use Continuous Innovation to Create Radically Successful Businesses*. New York: Crown Publishing.

Roos, Johan. 2017. Practical wisdom: making and teaching the governance case for sustainability. *Journal of Cleaner Production*. 140: 117-124.

Society for Interdisciplinary Studies. 2017. The Importance of Outsiders in Science. Accessed July 19, 2017. http://www.sis-group.org.uk/silver/newgrosh.htm

Tovstiga, G., & D. W. Birchall. 2005. *Capabilities for Strategic Advantage—Leading Through Technological Innovation*. Basingstoke: Palgrave Macmillan.

Wernerfelt, B. 1984. The Resource-Based View of the Firm. *Strategic Management Journal* 52: 171–180.

White, G. 2017, 04. Melinda Gates: The Tech Industry Needs to Fix Its Gender

Problem—Now. The Atlantic. Retrieved Sept. 29, 2017. http://www.theatlantic.com/business/archive/2017/03/melinda-gates-tech/519762/

Zhang , C. & Woodland, P. C. 2015. *Parameterised Sigmoid and ReLU Hidden Activation Functions for DNN Acoustic Modelling*. Cambridge, UK: Cambridge University Engineering Dept.

The Economist. July 15, 2017. The algorithm kingdom.

Tuckman, B. W. 1965. Developmental Sequence in Small Groups. *Psychological Bulletin*, 63 (6): 384–399.

Tuckman, B. W., & Jensen, M.A.C. 1977. Stages of Small Group Development Revisited. *Group and Organizational Studies*, 2, 419- 427.

ABOUT THE AUTHORS

Magnus Penker

Magnus Penker is an internationally renowned thought leader on innovation, digitization, and business transformation. He has spoken at prestigious global forums and events including the Global Peter Drucker Forum, top-ranked international business schools, a variety of associations, and some of the world's largest companies.

He has been honored with two Business Worldwide Magazine awards for his achievements, the "Most Innovative CEO Sweden 2016" and "Growth Strategy CEO of the Year Sweden 2016" awards. Additionally, he has launched ten start-ups and has acquired, turned around, and sold more than thirty European SMEs.

Through his best-selling American books on digitization and IT engineering, and his more than twenty years of experience as a management consultant and business leader, Mr. Penker inspires leaders to find a new way of thinking and organizing to stay on top.

For the past eight years, he has used his practical and theoretical insights to develop InnoSurvey, a leading methodology and global innovation database that is used for business analysis and support to companies, business leaders, and scientists around the world. Today, Mr. Penker is the CEO and founder of the Innovation360 Group, headquartered in Stockholm, Sweden, and New York in the United States.

Mr. Penker is driven by the recognition that in these turbulent times, we must understand our core strengths and determine how we can use those capabilities and competencies to create advantages in a globalized market with endless possibilities. The global map is being redrawn at speeds never before seen, and historically low interest rates are attracting capital to global digital-risk projects that will further strengthen this movement.

Mr. Penker has a BSc in Computer Science (CTH, Sweden) and an MBA from the Henley Business School, England.

Peter Junermark

Peter Junermark is an acclaimed trainer who has brought his skills to some of the world's most recognizable brands. As a leader of Innovation360 workshops, Peter specializes in bringing disruptive technology and breakthrough projects to life. He is the senior software architect and lead developer with primary responsibility for the platform supporting the tools of the Innovation360 Group.

Before joining the Innovation360 Group, Peter was cofounder and a senior manager at Open Training Sweden's Gothenburg office. During his long-term consultancy at the Volvo Information Technology headquarters, Peter built learning-management and competence-management systems.

As one of the initial contributors to the Innovation360 Framework, Peter brings to this series of volumes a deep understanding of the theoretical foundations of his work. Peter's training background and logically ordered thinking proved to be invaluable in explaining the most complex relationships in plain language with examples that are easy to visualize.

Peter holds a master of science in computer engineering from Chalmers University of Technology in Gothenburg, Sweden. His latest projects involve the investigation of cutting-edge AI that expand on agile methodologies and establish an easily sharable set of coding principles.

Sten Jacobson

Sten Jacobson has successfully managed more than two hundred management-consulting assignments, during which he challenged board members, executive teams, and managers to keep pressing for more creative yet profitable business models, often with sustainability at the core of the differentiation.

He is a master at the practical applications of Blue Ocean strategy creation, which is designed to unearth one-of-a-kind, data-derived pockets of uncontested markets. He shows companies how to redraw industry boundaries in such a way that it essentially makes competition irrelevant.

Sten is the leading instructor for the accreditation of Innovation360's global cadre of licensed practitioners. He has been instrumental in spreading the InnoSurvey results and methodologies out to every continent. He has engaged within workgroups at the ongoing international standardization work (ISO) on innovation-management systems and innovation-management assessment. Among Sten's most in-demand skills are his expertise in executive-team mentoring, power conceptualization/visualization, seismic disruption, and the applications of advanced tech within professional services. His speaking engagements for C-level execs and international associations also frequently center on his work in value-proposition design, business-process mapping, and digital transformation.

He brings to this series a wider perspective on strategic execution of Innovation360 principles, translating the mechanics of innovation into management standards and practices that can be put into effect the moment the innovation team is assembled.

Sten holds a master of science in electronic engineering from the Royal Institute of Technology (KTH) in Stockholm, Sweden. He also holds higher-management education from the Stockholm School of Economics (SSE) in Stockholm.